Managing Student Behavior

How to identify, understand, and defuse
challenging classroom situations.

Marsha Costello

Pembroke Publishers Limited

© 2022 Pembroke Publishers
538 Hood Road
Markham, Ontario, Canada L3R 3K9
www.pembrokepublishers.com

Library and Archives Canada Cataloguing in Publication

Title: Managing student behavior : how to identify, understand, and defuse challenging classroom situations / Marsha Costello.

Names: Costello, Marsha, author.

Identifiers: Canadiana (print) 20210394196 | Canadiana (ebook) 20210394242 | ISBN 9781551383552 (softcover) | ISBN 9781551389554 (PDF)

Subjects: LCSH: School discipline. | LCSH: Behavior modification. | LCSH: Classroom management.

Classification: LCC LB3011 .C67 2022 | DDC 371.102/4—dc23

Editor: Janice Dyer
Cover Design: John Zehethofer
Typesetting: Jay Tee Graphics Ltd.

Printed and bound in Canada
9 8 7 6 5 4 3 2 1

Contents

Preface

Managing student behavior is one of the most challenging things that you will face in the classroom. Student behavior can hijack an entire lesson, disrupt the learning of others, threaten the classroom environment, and lead to unsafe situations. It is important for you to be able to manage student behavior in a way that poses the least disruption to learning and instruction. The first step to successfully addressing student behavior is understanding the behavior and why it occurs.

Behavior is complex and managing behavior can be equally complex. But keep in mind that behavior happens for a reason. Behavior happens because it works—students get what they want by behaving in a particular way. For example, a student who curses at the teacher and is sent out of the room will continue to curse at the teacher if leaving the room is what the student is hoping to achieve. Behavior is maintained because it serves a purpose. Once you can identify the purpose, you can begin to alter the behavior. Sounds easy enough. But as you know, behavior modification takes time and commitment.

To address challenging behavior, you need limits and expectations that are clear and consistent. And you need to communicate as calmly and compassionately as you can. Clear and consistent limits and expectations must also be fair and realistic. These themes will come up multiple times throughout this book.

> **TIP** Establish clear and consistent limits and expectations that are fair and realistic.
> Communicate calmly and compassionately.

This book provides an in-depth understanding of behavior, including identifying factors that trigger and maintain behaviors. It offers an overview of reinforcement, which is fundamental for positive behavior changes, and highlights many effective and evidence-based strategies to support behavior modification.

We have included a range of examples and anecdotes throughout this book to help give insight into the many complexities of behavior, and strategies and approaches you can use to diffuse challenging situations. We also explore how positive relationships and interactions can support behavior management and how to successfully navigate challenging situations.

Chapter 1 provides an in-depth look at the complexities of behavior and helps you understand why behaviors occur. We look at the contributing factors of behavior and provide various examples to help put things into perspective. We also outline the steps for addressing problem behavior.

In Chapter 2, we explore how to create a plan to address behavior. We start by exploring the causes and function of behavior, then review how to create a behavior support plan and design behavior contracts. We also examine several factors to consider when addressing the functions of behavior.

Chapter 3 considers sensory difficulties (i.e., over- or under-stimulation). We explore the role of occupational therapists in helping students regulate their sensory responses and needs. We also provide a number of strategies to support students' sensory needs.

We examine the importance of respect and relationships in Chapter 4. We look at the importance of maintaining a calm approach as well as the benefit of finding common ground with a student. When we genuinely like our students, they will know this, and it will go a long way in helping deal with challenging behaviors.

Chapter 5 looks at regulation and co-regulation. Regulation can be very difficult for many students. You can help students develop their regulations skills by co-regulating with them. We explain not only the importance of this concept, but also provide insights and approaches to successfully co-regulate with and for your students.

Reinforcement is one of the biggest concepts in behavior management. Chapter 6 explores reinforcement, looking at what it is, how it works, and essential components of reinforcement. We provide multiple examples of reinforcement programs and how to use them.

Chapter 7 outlines the importance of data collection and provides multiple examples of data collection templates that can be individualized as needed. An explanation of each template is included, as well as considerations for what information is needed in various situations. We also look at tracking and monitoring behavior and using the data to inform next steps.

In Chapter 8 we review the importance of predictability for supporting behavior management, and we look at multiple ways to enhance predictability. We include examples of whole class and individual schedules, as well as how to use them. This chapter also considers proactive ways to manage unpredictable events, as well as ways to support students with activities that may be predictable but are out of routine.

In Chapter 9 we dive into visual supports. Visuals are huge in behavior support and this chapter explores many ways to incorporate visuals into your daily routine, including social stories and scripts. We also look at visuals that support student-specific programming and planning.

In Chapter 10 we outline multiple ways to use timers with your students individually, in groups, and as a whole class. We look at various types of timers and how to use them for reinforcement.

Chapter 11 provides some additional suggestions for addressing other types of challenging behavior like running and self-injurious behavior.

Finally, Chapter 12 concludes the book.

1

Understanding Behavior

As a teacher, you are an expert in curriculum, instruction, and learning. As you facilitate curriculum and learning on a daily basis, you must navigate student behavior issues as best you can. In fact, many teachers often become well-versed in some of the most common challenges. Although there is no way that you can be an expert in all aspects of student behavior, learning more about the causes and functions of behavior will help you better manage behavior issues in the classroom.

Keep in mind that students with the same issues or conditions do not always present with the same behaviors. For instance, a student with academic difficulties may become very quiet and "invisible" in class to avoid drawing attention to themselves and being noticed by the teacher. Another student could behave in the complete opposite way to get kicked out of the classroom so they do not have to face their struggles/challenges. Behavior is complex and can occur for a multitude of reasons.

The Behavior Cycle

To help you understand the complex nature of behavior, think about behavior as being part of a larger cycle, as illustrated in Figure 1.1.

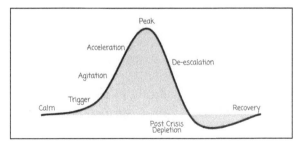

Source: https://hes-extraordinary.com/6-powerful-nvci-skills-for-handling-meltdowns

Figure 1.1: The behavior cycle

Although student behavior may appear to quickly escalate, there is generally a pattern to the escalation. As shown in Figure 1.1, something usually triggers a student to transition from a calm and productive state to an agitated state. It is sometimes difficult to recognize these triggers, but you can often determine them through data collection, which we will discuss in later chapters. An agitated state, if not settled, can escalate into a meltdown (peak). This is where you see the most challenging (and sometimes dangerous) behaviors, including flipping desks, physical aggression toward peers, staff, or self, and more. When the meltdown subsides (de-escalation), the student is often mentally and physically exhausted, described as post-crisis depletion. After a meltdown (recovery), students can experience feelings of guilt or shame. It is very important at this stage to rebuild a positive relationship with the student.

To successfully address challenging behaviors, you will need to understand the purpose behaviors serve in each stage of the cycle. This book will provide an in-depth look at each stage in the behavior cycle, as well as provide strategies and supports to respond to each stage.

This book will provide an in-depth look at each stage in the behavior cycle, as well as provide strategies and supports to respond to each stage.

Contributing Factors of Behavior

The factors discussed in this section are not exhaustive; in fact, they are just the tip of the iceberg.

> **TIP** Keep in mind that the diagnoses or root cause(s) of behavior help provide an understanding of why behaviors occur. But regardless of the diagnosis or root cause, you still need to consider and address the behaviors.

Medical Difficulties/Diagnosis

Vision and/or hearing problems, attention deficit hyperactivity disorder (ADHD), oppositional defiant disorder (ODD), fetal alcohol syndrome (FAS), autism, anxiety, chronic medical conditions, epilepsy, sensory needs, and more—multiple conditions can affect learning and/or behavior. This does not mean that students with these conditions should be permitted to misbehave because of their condition(s). Rather, you can use this information to anticipate challenging behaviors, understand why they are occurring, and proactively plan for them. Despite the presence/diagnosis of a condition, you can still address behavior in a positive and successful way.

Some conditions have overarching characteristics that are very common from student to student. For instance, ODD is characterized by oppositional behaviors such as refusal to follow requests or guidelines, being argumentative, and having negative responses to authority. ADHD also has common characteristics such as impulsivity, hyperactivity, and a short attention span. Though commonalities such as these exist, some characteristics are prevalent in more than one condition. For example, anxiety can present in a similar way to ADHD, but these two conditions are very different and your approach to each may differ. Therefore, it is important to look at the data (see Chapter 7) and consider all aspects of the student's profile when determining a course of action to address behavior.

Academic Struggles

Some students may believe they can't do the work or don't know how to do it. Others may be scared to try it or have accepted that they will never be able to do it. Students may struggle with non-preferred tasks or may have a learning disability in a particular area. In addition, absenteeism can create learning gaps. When students experience these types of academic challenges, they may engage in behavior to avoid academically demanding situations.

Sensory Difficulties

In basic terms, students may be over- or under-stimulated by their environments, which in turn can lead to problem behaviors. A student who is over-stimulated by their surroundings may tend to avoid activities and/or experiences with increased sensory input. Students who are under-stimulated by their environment may demonstrate increased or exaggerated responses to their environment.

Sensory difficulties can often be overlooked or misunderstood. Because these issues can have a significant impact on classroom behavior, we will explore them in more depth in Chapter 3.

Although the understanding of how adverse childhood experiences (ACEs) impact children first originated in 1995, it is still a relatively new concept for many educators. ACEs are common across all socioeconomic levels, with nearly two-thirds of the population experiencing some level of adverse childhood experiences. The more ACEs a child experiences, the greater their risk of life-long impacts.

More recent research demonstrates that the impact of ACEs can be reduced through positive childhood experiences (PCEs). The ACES Too High website (a news site that reports on PCEs and ACEs) states:

> This means that it's really important to have positive childhood experiences, no matter how much adversity you have in your life. And if you have a lot of adversity and a lot of positive childhood experiences, you are less likely to suffer the consequences of ACEs. However if you have no positive childhood experiences and few ACEs, the consequences of the ACEs are more likely to appear. (https://acestoohigh.com/got-your-ace-score/)

The importance of relationships cannot be understated and is a recurring theme throughout this book.

Having strong and positive relationships with your students contributes to positive childhood experiences and can help make a difference in terms of the impacts of ACEs. The importance of relationships cannot be understated and is a recurring theme throughout this book. (See the Recommended Resources section at the end of the book for more information about adverse childhood experiences and childhood trauma.)

Home Stress

Abuse, chronic illness, or death in the family, financial stress, substance use problems, mental health problems, separation/divorce—all these types of adverse childhood experiences can lead to behavior problems in the classroom. Abuse, neglect, and household challenges have an impact on children and have been linked to poor outcomes later in life, as well as poor academic achievement.

School Stress

Students may experience bullying, social media stress, limited/lack of friendships, social difficulties, personality conflict between student and teacher, limited supports and resources, lack of understanding of a learning/medical/behavioral condition, and more. This stress can lead to poor academic performance as well as an increase in disruptive behaviors. Although it is important to address behaviors as they occur, it is even more important to support students in reducing the stress they are experiencing so they can fully engage in their learning.

Trauma

Behavior stemming from childhood trauma is often the most difficult to address as it can take years for the student to get to a place where they are ready, able, and open to engage in meaningful learning (academic or otherwise). Trauma can be very complex and extremely challenging. Children who have experienced trauma can present as though they are significantly impacted by ADHD and even ODD. Receiving support from a trauma specialist is an important part of support for the student and the school team.

Steps for Addressing Problem Behavior

Regardless of the type of behavior you are trying to address, the approach will be the same:
- Meet with the school team.
- Complete any necessary assessments and/or referrals.
- Collect baseline data (this may happen before or after the meeting).
- Identify triggers.
- Identify possible reinforcers.
- Create a plan that considers
  ○ Alternate behaviors
  ○ Proactive strategies
  ○ Education and supports
  ○ Reinforcement
  ○ Consequences
- Collect data.
- Analyze data to determine if the strategies are working.
- Follow up with the team to review data and tweak the plan as needed.

The remainder of this book will provide information about this approach.

KEY IDEAS

- Behavior is complex and can occur for a multitude of reasons.
- To successfully address challenging behaviors, you will need to understand the purpose behaviors serve in each stage of the behavior cycle.
- Contributing factors of behavior can include medical difficulties/diagnosis, academic struggles, sensory difficulties, home stress, school stress, and trauma.

- The steps for addressing problem behavior include meeting with support staff, assessing and making referrals, collecting baseline data, identifying triggers and reinforcers, creating a plan, collecting data, analyzing data, and following up with support staff.

2

Creating a Plan to Address Behavior

A behavior support plan (BSP) is a detailed plan that addresses student behavior in a multi-tiered approach—education, remediation, skill development, proactive strategies, and consequence protocols. It includes developing strategies and recommendations for each of these areas. BSPs are created by a team and often require the support of multiple partners (e.g., guidance, community health, family counseling, teacher, support staff, resource, pediatrician, speech-language pathologist, occupational therapist, and more).

Behavior plans are an essential part of addressing challenging behaviors. The plan is designed specifically around the needs, interests, and behaviors of the student, and everyone involved needs to sign off on the final version. It outlines strategies and approaches to support growth and development, reinforce positive behaviors, and redirect negative behaviors. The team should regularly review the behavior support plan to ensure a consistent approach with the student as it keeps everyone on the same page.

Behavior plans are an essential part of addressing challenging behaviors.

Investigating the Causes of Behavior

The first step to creating a plan to address behavior is to investigate the causes of the behavior. Your resource/special education teacher and/or your school team should be your first contact. Collaborating with experts will help you gain the skills and knowledge you need to effectively address the challenging behaviors in your classroom.

It is likely that your school has a flow chart or list of steps to help determine the supports needed for students. This may include things like the following:

- Hearing and vision screens
- Review of the student's records/files if the teacher or the team is unfamiliar with the student and/or the student's background and history
- Possible assessments or observations
- Parent contact

- Consented contact with any specialists
- Case conference
- Data collection
- Creation of a behavior support plan (BSP)

Sometimes it is relatively easy to identify the cause of a behavior and rectify it. For example, consider this classroom situation:

> Suzie appears to be ignoring her teachers, and her teachers are starting to consider her as being oppositionally defiant. But in reality, Suzie is having issues with her hearing. A few hearing tests later, along with implementation of a personal FM system (i.e., frequency modulation system, a device that makes the teacher's voice more audible over other noises in the classroom), and the student's behaviors are averted.

Make sure not to overlook the "simple" things that can sometimes be the root causes of behaviors.

Although things don't usually work out that smoothly and easily in the real world, it's still very important to keep in mind that sometimes "simple" things are the root cause of behaviors and not overlook them.

> **TIP** Begin by considering and ruling out possible causes of behavior problems like hearing and vision problems, academic issues, hunger, sleep deprivation, and missed medications before considering more complex causes.

Consider another student, David, who is easily distracted:

> During math class he continuously watches the door and pays excessive attention to anyone walking by. Although you may be tempted to jump to the conclusion that David has ADHD, a team meeting reveals that there are significant financial issues at home and David comes to school hungry most mornings. Math class happens to be first thing in the morning. As academically capable as David may be, math does not compete with his need for breakfast. It turns out that David isn't distracted because of ADHD; he is waiting for the breakfast bin to arrive.

Again, this may not be the most common reason for distracted behavior, but for some schools and some populations, it's not implausible. Remember that not all behaviors are what they appear to be!

> **TIP** Reach out to school supports when you first start encountering challenging behavior to avoid becoming frustrated with the situation. Remember that every student has strengths, regardless of how challenging their behaviors may be.

The Function of Behavior

Even when the cause of a student's challenging behavior has been identified, it is important to determine the function of the behavior. For example, imagine you have a student in your class who is incredibly distracted, hyperactive, and impulsive. After multiple conversations and meetings with the parents and the school team, along with letters to the pediatrician, the student is diagnosed with ADHD. The student is also prescribed medication.

In the classroom, however, you are still experiencing some of those same challenging behaviors with the student. You may note a decrease in some behaviors, possibly resulting from medication, but some of the bigger problem areas persist. For a student with ADHD, it is likely safe to assume these include transition times, unstructured times (e.g., recess/lunch), gym class, and the bus ride to and from school. Why are these behaviors still occurring?

The most common reasons for challenging student behavior are escape, avoidance, attention, tangible, and sensory.

The most common reasons for challenging student behavior are escape, avoidance, attention, tangible, and sensory.

- **Escape** – When the student is faced with something they do not want to do or a situation they do not want to be in, they may behave in such a way to escape the task or situation. Consider an example: You put a math test on the student's desk. They flip their desk or call you an idiot, and you send them to the office. The result is that the student has successfully escaped the math test.
- **Avoidance** – This reason is similar to escape, except that the student knows the unwanted task/situation is coming so their behavior happens beforehand so they can avoid it altogether. Here's another over-simplified example: Language arts follows recess. The student struggles to read and write. They hate feeling stupid in front of their peers. They shove the students in the line-up on the way into school and they are sent to the office. In this way, they avoid language arts completely.
- **Attention** – For some students, the attention they get when they misbehave makes the behavior worthwhile. Students who misbehave for attention very rarely distinguish between positive and negative attention—any attention will do. For example: When the teacher reprimands a student and everyone is watching, they have an audience. This attention may be all that is needed to maintain the behavior.
- **Tangible** – In this situation, the child behaves in a certain way to obtain an object. For example: A child throws a temper-tantrum in the grocery store checkout line and the parent offers the child a box of Smarties to keep them quiet. In the simplest terms, tantrum in the checkout line = Smarties.
- **Sensory** – These behaviors serve a sensory need for the student. For example: A student may constantly rub or tap or bang, stomp instead of walk, or hurt their peers because they hug them too hard. These behaviors may not be for disruptive purposes or to be mean to peers, but instead they may serve a sensory need for the child.

Identifying the Function of Behavior

Sometimes the function of a student's behavior may be evident, like in the following examples.

- Colleen whispers "stupid" to Dell when he gets something wrong, so Dell punches her. Punching is not okay and will need to be addressed, but you can understand why this behavior occurs.
- Lynda's dog died last night; a peer does a book talk about Lassie, and Lynda runs from the room. Leaving the room without permission is not okay (usually), but you can see why this behavior happens.
- Lyla has been getting into fights all day with her peers. Her sister shares with the counselor that their parents separated last night. You need to address Lyla's behavior, but you can understand why social interactions are so hard for her today.

At other times it may be very difficult to determine the function of the behavior. You may need to gather data on the behavior (we will look at data collection in detail in Chapter 7) and possibly participate in a formal information gathering/analyzing process to determine the function of the student's behavior. Once all the information is collected, you can then analyze it by looking for patterns in terms of the time of day, day of the week, class/subject, task, transitions, and more.

When looking at data to determine the function of a behavior, it is important to have all the key players around the table. This includes the teacher, any support people, and the parent(s)/caregiver(s). Sometimes students may participate in a meeting depending on their age and ability, as well as the sensitivity of the information to be addressed. Participants can share their knowledge of the student and their experiences with the challenging behaviors. This process should cover a broad scope to give a detailed understanding of issues and contexts that may be supporting the behavior(s), including student strengths, background information, triggers, behaviors, and consequences. These elements become the foundation for the behavior support plan.

- **Strengths** – Includes anything that the student is good at (even relatively speaking). You can also include things the student likes. Beginning the meeting by focusing on strengths accomplishes two things: It allows you to identify possible reinforcers when looking at a behavior plan, and it sets a positive stage for discussing challenging behaviors.
- **Background Information** – Includes things that may contribute to a student's difficulties but that do not immediately precede the behavior, such as learning disabilities, medical diagnosis, social difficulties, family situation(s), and more. Background information, commonly referred to as slow triggers, includes things that are part of the student's context that may add to their stress level on any given day.
- **Triggers** – Unlike slow triggers, which are always part of a student's context, fast triggers are the things that immediately precede a behavior. Examples may include peer humiliations, task demands, being told "no," specific subjects, and more. Identifying the fast triggers that most commonly precede a behavior is important for addressing the behavior.
- **Behaviors** – Includes explicit and definable behaviors. Identifying that the student "melts down" or "gets upset" is not optimal as this looks different to different people. What one teacher might consider a meltdown could be viewed by another as "just blowing off steam." When defining behaviors, include specific actions like biting, kicking, cursing, slamming a fist into the desk, rolling eyes, spitting, etc. There are fewer misinterpretations when you define behaviors in

Consider the issues and contexts that may be supporting the behavior(s), including student strengths, background information, triggers, behaviors, and consequences.

very specific and explicit terms. This is especially important when multiple people are supporting and addressing the student's behavior.

- **Consequences** – Includes anything that occurs immediately after the behavior happens. You may think that consequence means punishment, but in reality, multiple consequences occur naturally following a behavior. For example, if the students in the class all gasp or laugh or fall silent, this is a consequence of the behavior. Similarly, if a peer laughs loudly or yells out "good one," this is a consequence of the behavior. If the student is addressed sternly by the teacher or is asked to leave the room, or if the teacher sends a note home or calls the parent(s), these are also consequences. Consequences can be very reinforcing for a student and often serve to maintain challenging behaviors. It is also important to note that peer consequences (e.g., laughing, giggling, gasping, etc.) provide attention. And, as we stated before, for many students seeking attention, there is no difference between good and bad attention.

For many students seeking attention, there is no difference between good and bad attention.

 TIP Many experts now refer to "attention seeking" as "connection seeking" or "relationship seeking" as this is more positive and creates a different understanding of the student and the behavior. We use "attention seeking" here only because that term is more common.

Creating a Behavior Support Plan

The data discussed above is then analyzed to identify any patterns that may be present. Patterns can involve key times when issues present, specific tasks that cause behavior outbursts, or consequences that appear to maintain the behavior (discussed further in Chapter 7). Once the data is analyzed, a behavior support plan (BSP) is created to outline the approach that will be taken to modify the challenging behavior(s).

The behavior support plan is created from the information discussed above. Each topic (i.e., strengths, background, triggers, behaviors, and consequences) becomes the basis for a section in the BSP.

- Strengths are used to identify objects and/or activities that would be reinforcing to the student. These are then built into the plan as scheduled opportunities and/or contingent reinforcement. Both types of support are beneficial. With scheduled reinforcement, the student has positive activities built right into their day. These occur according to the schedule and are not contingent on behaviors. Whether the student is having a good day or a not-so-good day, they still participate in these opportunities. With contingent reinforcement, the student receives reinforcement based on the presence or absence of specific targeted behavior. We discuss these further in Chapter 6.
- Supports address any areas of need that arise in the background section. These could include referrals to services such as a pediatrician, psychologist, speech pathologist or occupational therapist, family counseling, trauma support, and more. In-school supports such as academic assessment and/or intervention could also be included in this section to address academic gaps that may have been identified.
- Strategies are identified to help the student react more appropriately when they experience "triggers." These could be educational in nature and may involve

the guidance counselor, a school youth service worker, or even the resource teacher. Skills taught may include things like identifying bodily cues for stress/frustration, learning to ask for a break, deep breathing or relaxation techniques, and many more. Necessary materials might also be referenced in this section, like social stories, visuals, break cards, timers, etc.

- The behaviors are prioritized to determine which behavior to focus on first. It would be too overwhelming to try to tackle everything at once! You will also track behavior to make sure you are seeing a change in the right direction.
- Consequences are also used to help identify reinforcers. For example, if the data suggests that peer attention is maintaining negative behaviors, then build opportunities for positive peer attention into the plan.
- The plan includes a section that outlines the consequences for behaviors moving forward. This section is progressive and provides guidelines for how staff should respond to the various behaviors the student exhibits. For students who become violent or physically aggressive, it is important to include any physical intervention that may be necessary and to detail the logistics of this (e.g., when and why a restraint/hold might be necessary, who would perform this, required training, and any necessary follow up). It important to understand any guidelines/restrictions your district has in relation to physical interventions (i.e., restraints, holds, etc.) and ensure all involved staff understand them.

It may be useful to record "by who" and "by when" for any actionable items. For instance, if a referral to a pediatrician is part of the plan, document who is making the referral and when this is happening. This will help keep track of progress on all aspects of the plan. Frequent follow-up meetings are recommended, perhaps bi-weekly or monthly depending on the needs of the student and feasibility of such scheduling. Review how things are going, who has done what, challenges, and supports needed during the follow-up meetings. Reviewing data to ensure that behaviors are decreasing is also an important part of these meetings. We discuss this further in Chapter 6.

 TIP Behavior support plans are comprehensive. They are very detailed and outline a plan of action involving multiple support people. Reviewing the BSP with all parties involved, and having them sign the plan, is important to ensure everyone is aware of and agrees with the plan.

Designing Behavior Contracts

Depending on the age and cognitive ability of the student you are dealing with, there may be opportunities to use a behavior contract. Behavior contracts are agreements between the student and an agent of the school (e.g., teacher, guidance counselor, administrator, etc.). All parties need to agree to the terms of the contract. This allows the student to have some say and control over the contract, which can give them a sense of ownership over the agreement. When a student buys into a plan, the chance of success is greatly increased. A behavior contract traditionally outlines the student's obligation in terms of positive behaviors to increase and/or negative behaviors to decrease. It also contains the teacher's obligation to provide reinforcement contingent on the student meeting their obligation. Behavior contracts can be used with small groups or even the whole class, but typically they are used with individual students.

Having a positive relationship and/or rapport with the student goes a long way when crafting a behavior contract. There is an element of trust and vulnerability as both parties clearly articulate their terms, needs, and expectations. We look at relationships and rapport in Chapter 4. (See the Recommended Resources section at the end of the book for examples of behavior contract templates.)

Making the Function Functional

As we mentioned in Chapter 1, behavior happens because it works—students get what they want by behaving in a particular way. Once you know why the behaviors are occurring and which of the functions (i.e., escape, avoidance, attention, tangibles, or sensory) the behaviors are serving, you can look at alternate ways to achieve the same functions. If the student requires a BSP, this will make up a large component of the plan.

Addressing the Functions of Behavior

Remember, when you are dealing with significant behaviors, you are not alone. You have a school team to support you.

Note that in all the examples provided in this section, other supports may be in place depending on the issues the student is experiencing. Remember, when you are dealing with significant behaviors, you are not alone. You have a school team to support you.

Escape

If a student is exhibiting behaviors to escape a task or situation, offer them the opportunity to escape the task based on a very minimal expectation. Recall how we stressed the important of fair and realistic expectations in the Preface. This comes into play here. What you will expect from the student will depend heavily upon several things, such as:

- Age
- Ability (look past basic capabilities here and consider things like time of day, demands they have encountered thus far in the day, etc.)
- Current level of performance
- Other important factors

For example, consider this classroom situation:

Juanita has been demonstrating significant behaviors (i.e., desk flipping) each time she is given a math worksheet to complete independently. Math occurs early in the day, so she has not been overly taxed at this point. Although she has a history of poor performance in math, you believe she has skills and could be successful if you could get her to engage in the work.

START SMALL! Before even giving Juanita the worksheet, offer her the escape. Tell her that once she completes the first question (or circles a question on the paper, or picks a question, and so on), then she can leave. Offer her as much help as she needs to experience success—even though this is supposed to be an independent activity, it is important to focus on success. Praise her explicitly and let her go. Then the next day, aim for one question with less support required. Eventually you will increase your expectations, but for now you are working toward decreasing behaviors and building success. Math achievement will be a natural consequence.

Avoidance

Avoidance will happen in much the same way as escape. Offer the student the opportunity to get out of the task/situation based on small and realistic expectations.

Attention

To address attention-seeking behaviors, you need to give the student attention. First, minimize (often called ignoring) the attention you give to negative behaviors. You may need to have a chat with the other students about this as well. What you say will depend on the age and maturity of the class. You may also want to offer incentives to the class for ignoring inappropriate/negative behaviors (this will become clearer when we look at reinforcement in Chapter 6). Just remember, you are ignoring the behavior, not the student.

Ignoring can be hard to manage in the moment, and the idea of ignoring the behavior but not the student can be confusing. For instance, imagine you are doing a morning message and Micah is wandering around the classroom, knocking students' coats off their chairs. Inviting Micah to join the circle or directing him to come and sit down is appropriate, as it outlines what is expected of Micah but does not give attention to what Micah is doing. In contrast, pausing your morning message to engage with Micah about what he is doing or why he is doing it gives specific attention to Micah's behavior and provides him with a large audience.

Second, look for any and every opportunity to offer attention to the student for positive and appropriate behaviors. There are many ways you can offer attention. For instance, attempt to observe positive things occurring throughout the day and offer explicit praise and attention for them. Depending on the extent of the negative/inappropriate behaviors, provide additional attention for positive/appropriate behaviors. You can even get the class involved in praising the student and supporting their efforts. Imagine if you say, "Franco, I am so proud of how many times you raised your hand in class today! Let's all celebrate by going outside ten minutes early!" Peers will be very helpful in supporting Franco's positive behaviors when they get to participate in random acts of praise and celebration.

Tangibles

If you have a student who exhibits challenging behaviors to access something tangible, offer that same tangible thing for appropriate behaviors. For example, consider Kenita, a student who has been having meltdowns for several months:

> In an attempt to support Kenita, she is removed from the classroom when she has a meltdown and is taken to a sensory room to calm down. This plan is very well-intentioned and seems successful as Kenita always calms down in the sensory room. Despite this, Kenita's meltdowns become more frequent in class. Although this plan made sense at the time, Kenita has learned that she gets access to the sensory room by having meltdowns. She is now having more meltdowns because she likes going to the sensory room.
>
> In this situation, look at several different options including scheduled times for Kenita to access the sensory room, as well as random times she can earn access to

it based on positive and appropriate behavior. Scheduled times need to be routine and predictable and should be scheduled *before* Kenita would have been typically accessing the room. In this way you are being proactive and Kenita will learn that she does not have to "melt down" to access the sensory room.

Sensory

To address a sensory behavior, you need to find an alternate way for the student to receive the same (or a similar) sensory input. Consider a young student who rubs people's clothing, which can become awkward. Give the student a swatch of fabric samples on a ring to keep in their desk or pocket. In this way, the student can meet their sensory needs by rubbing the various samples rather than rubbing people's clothing. You could also try pairing the fabric ring with a social story to help explain why it is preferred that the student rub the swatches as opposed to people's clothing. (See Chapter 9 for more information about social stories; see Chapter 3 for more information about sensory issues.)

> **TIP** Your school resource/special education teacher or your school team can help identify replacement behaviors for sensory needs. They can also connect you with an occupational therapist (OT) who has experience working with sensory needs.

Targeting Behaviors

Once you have accurately determined the function of the behavior, you can begin to change the behavior by ensuring the student is able to achieve the same function but in more appropriate ways, as described briefly above. Although a student may have multiple challenging behaviors, it is important to tackle these one (or possibly two) at a time. Prioritize the behaviors considering things like safety and stigma (i.e., target behaviors that may be stigmatizing to the student, may hinder or inhibit friendships, or may cause them to be ostracized).

Tackle the biggest and most significant behaviors first.

Tackle the biggest and most significant behaviors first. This does not mean that you are not addressing other behaviors; it just means that you are purposefully targeting (planning and programming to reduce a specific behavior) one behavior at a time. For example, if the target behavior is biting, this does not mean that you are going to allow Donalda to say the "f" word and smear her lunch on her peers because you are only addressing biting. Instead, continue to re-direct and consequence those behaviors as you always did, while at the same time focusing on strategies in place to target biting.

> **TIP** Keep in mind that behavior change takes time. Don't be discouraged. Although at times you may believe that your "plan" is not working, it is difficult to make this conclusion unless you are collecting data (see Chapter 7). When targeting a behavior, look at the data to determine the success of your intervention(s). There may also be times when a plan doesn't work or success starts to slow down. If your data support these observations, review the plan and see if there are some changes that can be made.

Extinction Burst

When you begin to target any given behavior, you will notice a sudden and significant increase in that behavior. Believe it or not, this is a good sign. The extinction burst is the student's last-ditch effort to continue the behavior to meet their needs. For example, if you have a student who screams, expect them to scream louder and longer than ever before. If you have a student who hits, expect them to hit harder and more often. You will have to persevere through the extinction burst.

A good example is parents trying to get an infant to sleep through the night. The parents might make a purposeful decision to not go into the baby's room when they cry out. The result is that the infant usually cries longer and louder the first night. The parents may be tempted to throw in the towel, but in the end their perseverance usually pays off and the baby begins sleeping through the night. You will see these same gains when you address a student's behavior, but you will have to persevere through the extinction burst. It won't last long, but it will be intense.

Giving in to an extinction burst is a very big set back. It reaffirms for the student that their behaviors do in fact work and it reinforces the continuation of their behaviors. For instance, if you are targeting a student's ranting and part of the plan is to ignore the rant and redirect the student back to the task at hand, this will be new for the student. The student will be frustrated with the sudden ignoring of their rants. Suppose this student usually begins a rant prior to silent reading time and the rant usually ends with the student being removed from the classroom, the student's goal for this behavior. When you begin to ignore the rants, which had typically resulted in the student being removed, the student will be caught off guard and will rant louder and longer, possibly including profanity or more profanity than is typical. They are increasing their behavior to attain their goal of being removed from the classroom.

When they are not removed, they will continue to rant. If you give in at this point and remove the student, you have created a new threshold for their behavior. The next time you attempt to ignore the behavior, the student will easily jump to this new level and will then increase their behavior from there if you persist in your planned ignoring.

Triggers

Triggers are the things that precede the behaviors. They are the things that "set us off" in the moment. When you know your student's triggers, you are more readily able to help prevent challenging behaviors from occurring. Knowing the triggers allows you to intervene prior to a behavior.

There are many strategies you can use to support a student in an attempt to avoid a meltdown. Some of these may include:

- **Deep breathing** – A technique in which the student inhales and exhales in a deep and controlled manner.
- **Tense and release** – A technique in which the student squeezes their muscles and then relaxes them.
- **Progressive muscle relaxation** – A technique in which the student tenses and relaxes their muscle groups from head to toe, or vice versa.
- **Visualization** – Involves the student picturing a calm activity or picturing their "happy place."
- **Proprioceptive (deep pressure) activities** – These activities help ground energy levels and involve major muscle groups.

Although these strategies may be useful in preventing a meltdown or helping regain composure following a meltdown, this does not mean they are useful for stopping a meltdown while it is occurring. In the midst of a meltdown, the student is not cognitively or emotionally able to pause and try one of these strategies. As an example, think back to a time when you were extremely angry. You were probably not thinking about pausing your anger to do something productive. Instead, your instinct may have been to yell, slam a door, or walk away. The same applies to a student during a meltdown. The strategies listed here may further escalate the student in the midst of the meltdown.

Here is a classroom example:

> Shandi becomes extremely upset (e.g., covering her ears, dropping to the floor, rocking back and forth, and screaming) when loud and unanticipated noises happen. You can plan for that. Have a story or script prepared about unanticipated noises, have things like earplugs or noise cancelling headphones readily available and easily accessible, or identify items that are calming for her and make them available. You could also be proactive when possible and tell her when loud activities and events are upcoming. For example, take Shandi outside prior to the fire alarm so she hears it from farther away the first few times. You could even pre-expose Shandi to things that are going to occur, such as the volume associated with an upcoming assembly or a video in class.

Sometimes you don't know the actual trigger, but you know what behavior a student exhibits before they exhibit a more significant behavior. This can be as useful as knowing a trigger as it will still allow you to be proactive and intervene sooner. When you can intervene prior to a full escalation, you can often divert the full escalation. This is a success for everyone involved.

Consider another example:

> You know that before Ronald becomes physically aggressive, he often clenches and unclenches his fists and pulls at the collar of his shirt/sweater. Instead of needing to jump in between Ronald and a peer and engage in a restraint hold (which is never good for anyone involved), intervene when you see Ronald clenching his fists or pulling on his collar. For someone like Ronald, a BSP would contain de-escalation strategies for when he is fully escalated as well as strategies to intervene prior to a full escalation.
>
> As Ronald begins to experience success with proactive interventions, begin to work with him on self-identifying his body cues. He will begin to recognize when he is becoming upset and use the strategies independently. This will take time, but it will happen. Co-regulation will play a huge role in Ronald learning to self-regulate. (See Chapter 5 for more information about regulation and co-regulation).

De-escalation

As we have learned, despite your most effective strategies and your best intentions, meltdowns will still happen. How you support a student after a meltdown is very important. As shown in Figure 1.1, which shows the behavior cycle, after the peak stage comes de-escalation. De-escalation is the calming down process for a student who has become emotionally and/or behaviorally dysregulated (i.e., unable to manage emotional responses). De-escalation can look very different for each student and may depend on things like age, where they are in their

When you can intervene prior to a full escalation, you can often divert the full escalation.

behavior cycle, what things they respond to, recommendations in their behavior support plan (if applicable), and available resources.

Ideally, you want to proactively avoid behaviors when you can while still having students engaged, to the best of their abilities, in the task at hand. This is not always possible. Students don't usually go from being cooperative to melting down in one step. There is generally a progression of behavior in the cycle. Initially, expect to see the student becoming disengaged. It is important to respond in a supportive way when interacting with the student at this step. If the student is struggling with the task, provide the supports they need such as walking them through the task, helping them through the difficult part, or explaining something that may be causing an issue. At this stage you are providing them with skills and support that they need to try to address the cause of their disengagement.

Another strategy is offering the student a way out. For example, ask the student if they need a break or prompt them to use their break card (i.e., a strategy where the student uses cards or signals to alert the teacher to their need for a break). Suggest they complete a small amount of work (depending on the student and the task at hand, this could be finishing writing the sentence they are on, completing one more math problem, or reading to the end of the page) and then move to something else. By having the student complete a small amount of work, you are attempting to ensure that the student does not see their behavior as a way to get them out of the task at hand.

If this approach works, then the student will be back on track and all is well. Check in with the student a bit more frequently following this, and offer them a lot of praise for continuing with the task. It may also be beneficial to offer the student reinforcement at this point. For example:

> If you know that Ella loves stickers, bring a sticker to her desk and say something positive and explicit to her, such as "Ella I am really proud of you for working so hard on this. You didn't give up when it got hard. Good for you!" as you give her the sticker.

If your supportive approach does not work, then expect the student to become more emotionally charged. This may look like frustration, or the student may appear confrontational. Be clear and explicit in your expectations and become more directive with the student. It is important to note that although you are taking a directive approach, you need to try to remain emotionally neutral. You do not want the student to perceive you as becoming angry or frustrated.

In this phase, redirect the student to the task at hand. You can still offer support and a way out as discussed earlier, but you will do so in a more direct way. For example:

> Say something like, "Ella, you still need to complete two more problems before putting your math away. Once you're finished your math you can choose an activity from your list." If Ella is demanding something in particular or making statements of refusal such as "I don't care," "this is stupid," "I'm not doing any more," or "I hate this stupid class," be direct with her and say something like, "Yes, you can have computer time when you finish your story."
>
> You may feel like you don't want to "reward" Ella with computer time if she is being defiant. Presumably Ella has behavioral issues that you have been working on. Perhaps in the past Ella yelled "I hate this stupid class," threw her book at the white board at the front of the room, and ran out of the class. It is possible that in this scenario she never returned to the task she had been engaged with and simply

rejoined class when she was ready and started whatever activity was occurring at that time. If, instead, you can have Ella complete her task (even if you have decreased the expectations due to behavior) and then she earns computer time, this is a win. You have avoided the book throwing and her leaving the room, you have moved past the defiance to have her complete the task, and you now have something to praise and reinforce her for.

However, it is also possible that you don't win this one. Perhaps your directive approach is not successful. You would then expect to see the height of Ella's behaviors. You attempt to direct her to complete an abbreviated version of the task and have some computer time, but she yells, "I don't want the stupid computer!," throws her book, and runs from class. Ella will need to calm down before returning to class. She may have deep breathing, muscle relaxation, or visualization strategies that will be useful when she is ready. If she is in the midst of melting down, do not prompt these strategies. Instead, ensure that she is safe and that her behaviors are not jeopardizing her safety or that of anyone else.

Removing a student's peers from the room may be necessary. This removes an audience (if attention is reinforcing for the student) but also removes the students from a situation that may be very stressful and uncomfortable for them. In addition, it eliminates the possibility of anyone getting hurt should the student become physically upset. Another benefit of removing the students from the classroom is that it provides privacy and respect for the student while they are not able to control their emotional state. This may help reduce some of the embarrassment they may feel when they are calm and re-engage with the class.

> **TIP** If safety becomes an issue, physical restraint may be necessary. School districts and boards have policies and guidelines regarding physical restraint. There may be specific staff in your building trained to provide physical restraint if required. If you feel your student is heading down that path, discuss it with your resource teacher or school team.

How do you help a student who is having a meltdown return to a calm and functional way of being? There is no simple answer. Jody Carrington, child psychologist, provides some good advice: "You can't swallow when your lid is flipped." So, try offering the student a drink of water after they have had a meltdown. Drinking helps them "come back online," as Carrington puts it.

When the meltdown is over and the student is returning to a more emotionally regulated state, they may experience feelings of embarrassment or shame. It may be difficult for them to face you, or their peers after a meltdown. Some students may even prefer/benefit from a few minutes alone just to process the situation and regain their composure.

> **TIP** It is important to identify what de-escalation strategies work best for each individual student. An occupational therapist can be a great support in helping to identify which strategies may be most beneficial. In addition, a number of training programs are available to help teachers learn strategies for how to respond to students throughout the behavior cycle (e.g., Nonviolent Crisis Intervention®).

Your approach at this point needs to be positive and supportive. You want the student back in class and you want them to experience success.

As a student is calming down, it may be beneficial to praise them for calming down. This is not the time to delve into what happened, but rather to foster a calm and safe environment where they can emotionally rebound from their meltdown. Ensure that they feel welcomed back into the classroom. Rebuilding rapport is very important at this stage.

> **TIP** Remember that meltdowns are hard on everyone involved. Make sure that you are supported and know that your student's meltdown does not mean that you failed. Some meltdowns are unavoidable no matter how hard you try.

It will be important to debrief with your school team following a meltdown. The team will help determine if there are other strategies or recommendations to address the various levels in the student's behavior cycle.

KEY IDEAS

- A behavior support plan (BSP) is a detailed plan that addresses student behavior in a multi-tiered approach—education, remediation, skill development, proactive strategies, and consequence protocols.
- Reach out to school supports when you first start encountering challenging behavior to avoid becoming frustrated with the situation.
- You may need to collect data to determine the function of behavior: escape, avoidance, attention, tangible, or sensory.
- Consider the student's strengths, background information, triggers, behaviors, and consequences when identifying the function of behavior and creating a behavior support plan.
- Behavior contracts can allow the student to have some say and control, which can give them a sense of ownership over the agreement.
- Once you have accurately determined the function of the behavior, you can begin to change the behavior by ensuring the student is able to achieve the same function but in more appropriate ways.
- Tackle the biggest and most significant behaviors first.
- Make sure to persevere through extinction bursts, a sudden increase in the targeted behavior.
- Identify the triggers that lead to a behavior so you can intervene prior to a behavior.
- De-escalation is the calming down process for a student who has become emotionally and/or behaviorally dysregulated.
- Identify which de-escalation strategies work best for each individual student.

3

Sensory Difficulties

We refer to sensory needs and occupational therapists throughout this book, but you may not be overly familiar with these concepts. A deeper look at sensory difficulties may be useful in supporting student with these specific needs. Let's first look at a definition of sensory needs:

> Sensory issues occur when a child has a difficult time receiving and responding to information from their senses. Children who have sensory issues may have an aversion to anything that triggers their senses, such as light, sound, touch, taste, or smell. (https://www.healthline.com/health/childrens-health/sensory-issues-in-children)

In other words, students may be over- or under-stimulated by their environments, leading to problem behaviors.

Over-stimulation

A student who is over-stimulated by their surroundings may tend to avoid activities and/or experiences with increased sensory input. In the classroom, students may cover their ears or complain about volume, even when you do not think things are overly loud. Some students may find the lights too bright or struggle with the lights, volume, and echoes in the gym. They may also have an aversion to touch, suggesting someone "hit them" or "pushed them" when in fact there was only a touch or a brushing of shoulders. Other students may squirm or appear to be in discomfort because their clothing feels "too tight" or fabrics are too itchy and/or prickly.

Other behaviors that may occur due to over-stimulation (hyper-arousal) include (Amy Buie, *Rage to Reason*):
- Inability to focus or sit still
- Unable to follow rules
- Aggressiveness

A student who is over-stimulated by their surroundings may tend to avoid activities and/or experiences with increased sensory input.

- Resistance to directives
- Argumentative
- Anxiety before tests
- Impulsiveness
- Risk-taking behavior

Consider the following example:

Maximus is overly sensitive to volume. This shows up the most on the bus, which makes sense as the bus tends to be louder than other settings he interacts with. Maximus is generally able to tolerate his environment, but he struggles when he is having a bad day. Although he "tolerates" these situations, he is never comfortable with the volume on the bus. On a good day he can complete the bus ride without responding negatively or inappropriately to the noise.

Because of Maximus' home context, many of his days start on a rough note. Both his parents work, and consequently there are many mornings when one of his siblings is tasked with getting him ready for school. This results in him getting woken up later than usual, not having time to complete his morning routines, skipping a step in his routine, not having breakfast, or not having breakfast the way he wants.

On mornings when Maximus is already a little frustrated, he no sooner sets his foot on the first step of the bus when he begins yelling "Shut up!" This is not usually directed at any specific student, but to the bus in general. There are also times when he uses profanity, or when he stomps, slams, or throws things in response to the noise. Maximus has also been physically aggressive with peers if they are too loud for him.

Through conversations with his parents and the bus driver, the school team puts some strategies in place to support Maximus. They make a referral to an occupational therapist in the hopes of decreasing Maximus' aversion to volume (or increasing his tolerance). In the meantime, the bus driver gauges Maximus' mornings as he approaches the driveway. If Maximus is standing independently at the end of the driveway waiting for the bus, he is likely having a good morning. Likewise, if he is standing with one of his parents, this too is an indication that his morning has been good. In contrast, if Maximus is stomping around the driveway or yelling, that is a clear indication that his morning has been rough. And if he only runs out the door as the bus arrives, this too suggests that his schedule is off and his morning has not been not typical.

On these mornings, the bus driver makes a concerted effort to interact with Maximus before he steps foot on the bus. He spoke to the other students on the bus about volume when he first became aware of Maximus' aversion to noise, and he again prompts them to decrease their volume levels as he approaches Maximus' driveway. The driver greets Maximus in a calm and friendly voice. Some days he asks Maximus to help him with something. Because Maximus likes being a helper, this can help distract him from the noise levels on the bus.

The support staff post visuals on the bus wall by Maximus' seat to help prompt him to use his strategies and to keep his hands to himself. This consists of a few images and simple phrases that communicate that when the bus is too loud, he can put his schoolbag on the seat so no one sits with him, he can put on his noise canceling headphones, or he can listen to music. Maximus' parents supply an electronic device that stays in his schoolbag throughout the day, but that he uses on the bus to listen to music or play games. Maximus also sits at the front of the bus where the bus driver can keep an eye on him and engage in positive interactions during the bus ride.

Many students struggle to control their behavior while on the bus. And like Maximus, this can cause negative or inappropriate behaviors. Your school team can help determine appropriate strategies to address this issue. Visuals, alternate sensory input (like music for Maximus), and fidget toys can be useful. A bus buddy or bus job, when possible, can also be helpful. The strategies selected will depend on the needs of the particular student.

Under-stimulation

Students who are under-stimulated by their environment may demonstrate increased or exaggerated responses to their environment.

Students who are under-stimulated by their environment may demonstrate increased or exaggerated responses to their environment. In the classroom, students may yell or be unable to walk from one point to another without bumping, stomping, or twirling. Students may slam into their peers in line or crush them with hugs and squeezes that hurt or are uncomfortably hard. Other students may climb and jump off things or may appear to enjoy bumping into the walls and furniture. Students who are always tumbling and rolling around on the floor or crawling around or squeezing into small spaces (e.g., under desks, into bottom shelves, etc.) may be engaging in these behaviors as an attempt to seek input from their environments.

Teachers often wonder if students with these types of sensory problems have issues with impulsivity or hyperactivity. It will be important to tease this out as a student with ADHD exhibits behaviors as suggested here for very different reasons than one with sensory issues. The student with ADHD may be engaging in these behaviors because they cannot maintain their attention and have trouble staying focused and sitting still, whereas the student with sensory difficulties may be seeking sensory input.

Other behaviors associated with under-stimulation (hypo-arousal) include (Amy Buie, *Rage to Reason*):
- Defiance
- Withdrawal from peers
- Tardiness
- Absenteeism
- Shutting down (disassociation)
- Avoidance of tasks
- Numbing out ("I don't care")
- Forgetfulness

> **TIP** Working with your school team and the student's family is very important. The family may need to pursue medical advice to help determine the underlying cause of the student's behavior. This will ensure that strategies and recommendations appropriately address the issue. In some jurisdictions, this will require a referral to a pediatrician, and that can take months. In the meantime, put some strategies in place to try to support the student. Working with your school team and/or an occupational therapist is an appropriate next step while waiting for medical results or a possible diagnosis.

The Role of Occupational Therapists

Occupational therapists (OTs) are health care professionals who work with people of all ages (from infancy to death). Although the word "occupational" often gives people the idea that OTs have something to do specifically with a job or occupation, this is inaccurate. An occupational therapist helps individuals function within their environments, wherever that may be (e.g., home, school, work, leisure, etc.). OTs observe individuals in their environment to determine needed supports.

OTs address a vast range of issues including, but not limited to (https://www.webmd.com/pain-management/occupationalrehab#091e9c5e8134d0df-1-4):

- Prescribing and training people to use assistive devices like raised toilet seats or wheelchairs
- Teaching new ways to button a shirt, tie shoes, get in and out of the shower, or work on the computer
- Helping older adults prevent falls in their home or in public areas
- Treating adults who have had a stroke to improve balance, change their home to prevent injuries, build muscle strength, or adapt to their memory or speech problems
- Organizing medications or household tools
- Addressing behavior problems in children who act out or hit others
- Building hand-eye coordination so a person can hit a tennis ball
- Working on motor skills so a person can grasp a pencil

Collaborating with OTs can involve looking at the data together, doing paired observations when necessary, and brainstorming solutions and strategies.

For the purposes of this book, we will be looking at the role OTs play in supporting students with challenging behaviors. Collaborating with OTs can involve looking at the data together, doing paired observations when necessary, and brainstorming solutions and strategies.

Strategies to Support Sensory Needs

Sensory needs can be looked at in terms of eight main categories (https://www.healthline.com/health/childrens-health/sensory-issues-in-children#sensory-processing):

- **Proprioception** – The body's sense of awareness of its location, movements, and actions
- **Vestibular** – Inner ear spatial recognition that helps keep you balanced and coordinated
- **Interoception** – The sense of how you "feel," including temperature and emotions
- **Five senses** – Touch, hearing, taste, smell, and sight

If you know when these types of behaviors are occurring, make sure to implement strategies before the behavior occurs.

OTs observe and assess students' needs to determine which areas they are struggling with and how to best target the areas of difficulty. They use many strategies to help students regulate their sensory responses/needs. It is important to remain realistic in your expectations. Like anything else, these strategies will not result in the abrupt end of problem behaviors. If something is working, you will likely see a gradual decline in problem behaviors. And if behaviors dissipate more quickly than expected, that's great.

An important piece of targeting behaviors is timing. If you know when these types of behaviors are occurring, make sure to implement strategies before the behavior occurs. The intent is to provide the student with the sensory input they need before they begin to seek it in less appropriate or desirable ways. For instance, if a student comes in from recess flipping and spinning and slamming and banging, put sensory activities in place immediately following recess to help support them before they bang their way through your classroom.

A program called "Focus on Self-Regulation" is very useful for targeting many challenging behaviors (https://www.ecsd.net/page/1833/focus-on-self-regulation). The sequence to this program guides students through a series of activities intended to help them regulate their bodies. Applying this sequence immediately following recess would be a great way to support the student described above. This sequence can also be used with a small group of students before activities that they find challenging to help regulate them before they begin (e.g., before going to gym). For some students, it may be useful to do the focus sequence before *and* after specific activities. As always, you will be better able to make this decision depending on what works best for you and your student.

Sensory Rooms

Some schools have created sensory spaces (also known as sensory rooms or Snoezelen rooms) where students can relax and explore things that stimulate their senses. The concept of Snoezelen rooms began in Holland in the 1970s (https://www.abilities.ca/health-activity/snoezelen-rooms/). These rooms include items or activities that stimulate sight, touch, sound, and smell:
- Many are painted a dark color and contain various lighted objects (e.g., lava lamp, light strips, light up objects/gadgets, etc.) that the student can control.
- Sight is stimulated with mirrors, pictures, and other visual elements.
- Touch is stimulated with items of various textures, such as objects that are sticky, squeezable, soft, fluffy, powdery, and more, along with water and/or sand activities.
- Larger "touch" items are often included, such as hammocks, skipping ropes, and even swings.

- Sound stimulation is achieved through music or sound clips, echo and sound devices/gadgets, and even fans. Fans can also stimulate touch when they blow on the student, or sight when attached tassels move when fans are on.

> **TIP** Although sensory rooms have gained popularity over time, we are seeing a decrease in these spaces in schools for a variety of reasons. Check with your district to understand guidelines or restrictions in place in your area.

Note that many strategies incorporate sensory stimulation in the classroom.

Note that many strategies incorporate sensory stimulation in the classroom. This promotes inclusion while at the same time providing students with the sensory input necessary to succeed in their classroom environments—our ultimate goal.

Time-out Rooms

Like sensory rooms, many schools have time-out spaces or rooms that provide an under-stimulating environment. Students spend a set amount of time there as a consequence for negative behavior. In some instances, a time-out space is a chair facing into the corner at the end of a hallway. Time-out rooms serve the purpose of removing the student from the class and/or activity for a specific amount of time.

There are often explicit expectations for students while they are in a time out, including things like:
- remaining in their seat;
- not making noises; and
- complying with time-out rules for the duration of their set time.

> **TIP** Many jurisdictions have moved away from time-out spaces or have put strict guidelines in place for their use. These include not only expectations for use, but also templates for mandatory data tracking of time outs. If you or your school use time outs as a form of behavior management, make sure you are complying with any district/board mandates.

You may want to consider if using a time-out space will have the long-term impact you are hoping for. A time-out room removes the child from your class and provides you and the other students with a potentially much-needed break. But are there other ways to achieve a break that may be less isolating for the individual involved?

Some educators equate a time-out space with sending a child to their bedroom at home. But these two situations may not be the same. When parents send a child to their bedroom, they are not sending them to a space devoid of stimulation. Instead, parents are sending the child to a space that very likely contains some of their most comforting items/objects (e.g., pictures, their favorite stuffy, a place to curl up, a pillow to cry into, etc.). And often parents send the child to their room for a very short amount of time, just long enough to remove them from an audience or activity so they have time to process what just occurred. Parents often then talk with the child, in a calm and compassionate way, about what transpired, and possibly give them a hug and kiss as they leave the space together.

It is evident that facing a wall in a corner and having to sit still and not make noise for a set amount of time is different from sending a child to their room at home. For example, the relationship repair that often occurs with a child being sent to their room often doesn't occur with sending a student to a time-out space. In addition, when parents send their child to their room at home, they are not risking embarrassment or judgment from their peers.

Alternate Time-out Strategies

There are many other ways to achieve a time out without a formal time-out space. One of the biggest advantages to using alternate forms of time out is that they can be done in a positive and productive way to normalize the need for many students to take a time out from an activity to regain their bearings. And often these alternate methods do not risk damaging the relationship you have with your student, or the relationships between the student and their peers.

- **Head down** – Depending on the age and grade of the student, having them put their head on their desk for a short amount of time can serve as a time out. It removes some stimulation (with their head down they are not seeing everything going on) and can provide an opportunity for them to calm down. Having students put their head down for a brief amount of time is a common practice in many classrooms, so this may be less isolating and less stigmatizing than a formal time-out space. In some classrooms, teachers will pause an activity and have everyone put their heads down for a brief amount of time to help reset the energy in the room.
- **Seat away** – In some instances, again more common with younger grades, having the student sit at their desk, or at a seat away from an activity, for a short amount of time may remove them from stimulation and give them the opportunity to calm down. Once they are calm, they can return to the activity. Again, this is likely a routine practice in the classroom and therefore one that will be less likely to result in feelings of isolation or stigma.
- **Calm-down corner** – Some classrooms have a space that is referred to as a calm-down corner. Unlike a time-out space, this area contains items or visuals that are intended to help the child reduce their energy levels and/or return to a calmer state of being. These could include squeeze toys, stretch bands, or visuals to support calming strategies. The visuals and strategies would have been taught to the class and practised individually, in small groups, and as an entire class. In this way, students can employ the strategies independently when they are in the space.

Figure 3.1 (on the next page) shows one method to support students with calming down. You can use this strategy as a transition between activities and to calm restless students.

One of the biggest advantages to using alternate forms of time out is that they can be done in a positive and productive way to normalize the need for many students to take a time out from an activity to regain their bearings.

Brake:	Breathe:	Brain:	Body:
Put the "brakes" on excess energy.	Help regulate the central nervous system.	"Wake up" the brain.	"Wake up" the muscles and nerves in the body.
• Press your hands together firmly for 3–5 seconds. • Repeat 3 times.	• Place hands over belly button and take 3–5 deep, slow breaths. • When you breathe in, fill your belly with air so your hands push outwards.	• Interlace fingers and gently press down on your head 10 times. • Do the same on all sides of your head.	• Firmly apply pressure to your arms and shoulders.

Source: Adapted from https://omazingkidsyoga.files.wordpress.com/2011/11/4-bs-of-self-control-a-4-step-method-for-relaxing-tension-refocusing-calming.pdf

Figure 3.1 The 4B's of Self Control

- **Time out from an object/item** – It is also possible to have the student receive a time out from a specific object or item without having to leave the room or be removed from the activity. If a student flings an object being used in a learning activity across their desk or throws it at their peers, remove the object for an appropriate amount of time and then give it back with verbal direction regarding expectations. This gives the student a time out from the object but not from the learning activity. You could say something like, "Okay Maria, are you ready to use the object properly?" or "Okay Maria, let me see how you would use the object in the activity." You may choose to stay close to Maria for a short time and gradually move back to a more central location in the classroom as she demonstrates appropriate use of the object. Giving the object back also allows her to rejoin the activity and, hopefully, meet with success before moving on to another activity.

- **A walk** – For some students, remaining in the class may not be a productive place for them to calm down. In this situation it may be appropriate to have them go for a walk (this will depend on the ability of the child to do this independently, unless they have a support person who is able to monitor them). One of the best approaches is to send the student to the water fountain. This serves several purposes: It removes them from the class, it maps out a destination for their walk, and having a drink is calming. Having a student go for a walk is also likely a common practice in the classroom so it is not isolating or stigmatizing.

- **A break** – Offering the student the opportunity to take a break is another option. For some students, using a break card may already be part of the planning and programming in place for them. A break can look very different depending on the student. For some, it can be as simple as going to the water fountain. Others may leave the classroom for a few minutes and return. Some schools have chosen to create a sensory path in a quiet hallway that students can follow if they wish. The path consists of numbers, letters, shapes, and pictures that students follow—hopping, stepping, and jumping throughout.

- **An errand** – Having the student run an errand for you provides them with a break from the class/activity. Most students like to be helpful, so giving them a positive and productive reason to leave the class is more advantageous than sending them out of the room as a consequence. Also, it would be beneficial if your errand can involve the student carrying something heavy to someone/somewhere else (e.g., books to the library, paper to the administrative assistant, etc.) as carrying heavy objects can help ground their energy levels.

- **Alternate work locations** – Depending on the student, their age, and their abilities, it may be possible to offer them another place to work. In some classes this could mean an area close by (e.g., a teacher planning space off the classroom or a cubicle area at the back of the room). In other cases it may mean leaving the classroom (e.g., working in the library, the resource room, or an administrator's office). Regardless of the destination, the student would need to recognize these spaces as supportive places to work and not as places of punishment.

Some students may find it helpful to leave the room when they are overly distracted or when their energy levels are getting the best of them.

Some students may find it helpful to leave the room when they are overly distracted or when their energy levels are getting the best of them. These students might ask to work in the hallway or in another space close to the classroom. In these areas, the students can sprawl out on the floor and do their work. Make sure to keep students in your sightlines and that they do not block off the flow of traffic. You can incorporate these spaces into your group work locations at other times to normalize students working there.

Strategies for Outdoor Time Outs

Time outs can be necessary when students are outside at recess/lunch. Sending a student in from outside play could be comparable to a formal time out as it completely removes the student from the area and/or activity. However, this also limits any positive interaction between the teacher and the student and can be stigmatizing for the student. Although there may be times when sending the child inside is unavoidable, there are alternatives to sending students inside when their behavior does not warrant a full removal.

Although there may be times when sending the child inside is unavoidable, there are alternatives to sending students inside when their behavior does not warrant a full removal.

- **Redirecting activities or locations** – These involve directing the student to play with another student or group of students or directing them to play in another area. Both of these alternatives remove the student from specific peers and/or activities, but allow them the opportunity to stay outside and experience success in other ways.
- **Walking with the duty teacher** – Students could also be directed to walk with the duty teacher or playground supervisor for a set period of time. This allows the student to cool down and possibly discuss the situation before returning to the activity or joining a new activity. The duty teacher can gauge the energy level of the student and their mindset before determining next steps. In some instances, the student may only spend a brief amount of time with the teacher; in others, they may spend the rest of the break walking with the teacher.
- **Pairing peers** – There may be times when the duty teacher or playground supervisor identifies two students who are struggling. Having both students walk with the duty teacher may allow them to gain an understanding of their own behaviors by listening to the conversations between the teacher and the peer. It may also introduce the student to a peer with whom they share similarities, and it may provide a "friend" for the remainder of the break. The teacher can direct the two peers to play together and check back in with them at the end of the break.

Tactile Strategies

The mouth and the feet are sensory-rich parts of the human body. As a result, many students with sensory difficulties benefit from tactile strategies involving these parts of the body.

Some experts believe that oral sensory input is the quickest way to regulate the sensory system. Activities can be alerting or calming depending on the child, since everyone processes sensory input differently. For instance, an over-stimulated student could sink their teeth into a squishy ball for sensory release, while an under-stimulated student could do the same but as a way to become more alert.

The sensory systems in the mouth can serve several purposes:

- Sucking is soothing. This makes sense when you think about young children with soothers or sucking their thumbs.
- Chewing is organizational. Many people, adults included, chew on their pens or chew gum while they are working.
- Crunching is alerting.

Many teachers are open to the idea of allowing students to chew gum as a way to regulate the sensory system, provided they do not "see" or "hear" the gum. In other words, the gum always stays in the student's mouth—no bubbles, no twirling it on fingers, no sticking it in places (underside of desk/chair), and no noises such as smacking, snapping, or bubble popping. Chewing gum can help students organize their thoughts and better focus on the task at hand.

The feet, especially the soles of the feet, have multiple sensory receptors. As a result, walking and playing barefoot allow the muscles and the joints to react to changing surfaces, textures, and temperatures. This, in turn, supports sensory development. Other strategies involving the feet, like rolling a socked foot back and forth over a tennis ball, can help a student calm restlessness, organize their thoughts, and focus on the task at hand. This is a great strategy provided your student can control the ball and quickly slip on their shoe in the event of a fire drill. The tennis ball strategy is one that is not overly obvious to others and allows the student to continue working at their desk. Make sure to determine your student's ability to do this activity without losing the ball and having to chase after it or kicking it across the classroom.

KEY IDEAS

- Students with sensory difficulties may be over- or under-stimulated by their environments, leading to problem behaviors.
- Students who are over-stimulated by their surroundings may tend to avoid activities and/or experiences with increased sensory input.
- Students who are under-stimulated by their environment may demonstrate increased or exaggerated responses to their environment.
- OTs observe and assess students' needs to determine which area(s) they are struggling with and how to best target the area(s) of difficulty.
- Strategies to support students with sensory difficulties include using sensory rooms, time-out rooms, other forms of time out, and tactile strategies.

4

The Role of Respect and Relationships

Relationships and rapport are important aspects of behavior management. Establishing and maintaining positive relationships with students who challenge you the most can be difficult. Feeling constantly challenged, defied, and told off is not conducive to relationship building. Therefore, it is important to try not to take student behavior personally.

Jody Carrington, an internationally renowned child psychologist, stresses that the students we struggle with the most are the ones who are the most astute in terms of how the adults in their lives feel about them. These students have an instinct or intuition about the adults in their lives. Given this, it is important to be genuine with your students—if you honestly like them, they will be able to tell.

> **TIP** Behaviors are complex and they can feel very personal. Try to remain as emotionally disconnected from behaviors as you can. Students are not doing these behaviors to you or at you; they have a much deeper function. If you engage in these behaviors on an emotional level, it will be much more difficult for you to address them effectively.

Redefining Rude

Many educators feel that it is rude or mean to be direct with a student. But being direct does not have to be mean or rude; instead, think of it as being clear and explicit.

Consider the following classroom situation involving a teacher and a student with autism spectrum disorder (ASD):

> The teacher says, "James, honey, do you want to turn the lights off?" James says, "nope" and continues working on the task at hand. The teacher is appalled that he

is so rude and defiant. But as a student with autism, James tends to be very black and white. She *asked* him if he *wanted* to turn the lights off and he answered her honestly: He did not want to turn the lights off. "But I even said 'honey,'" the teacher says. That doesn't change the fact that she asked him a question and he provided her with an honest answer. "Well, I can't just *tell* him to turn the lights off! That would be rude." There is nothing fundamentally rude about giving a direction if you are polite and respectful.

Instead, be clear and explicit with your requests. The teacher says, "James, turn the lights off for me, please." James hops up out of his seat, turns the lights off, and returns to the task at hand. James does not respond to the direction to turn the lights off in a negative way. He does not perceive the direction as rude. Similarly, James is not defiant nor rude as the teacher had initially thought. James has autism. Understanding your students goes a long way to developing a positive rapport with them.

As a side note, if James didn't want to turn the light off (or on or anything else), does it really matter? Is this situation worth expending energy on? Does the teacher need him to do this for some reason? The teacher may believe that because all the other students love to turn the lights on and off, it would be unfair if she didn't give James the same opportunity. But it is not unfair to not ask him if he does not like doing it.

Another example might involve directing a student to sit in her seat. You may feel rude just telling her to sit down, believing that it seems bossy. But providing clear and explicit directions is not bossy or rude. For a primary grade student, you could say, for example, "Atia, honey, bum in your seat please."

> **TIP** Although you may be tempted to view students who exhibit extreme behaviors as manipulative or delinquent, this is not the case. Instead, they have learned to meet their needs through these challenging behaviors. Your goal is to teach them new and more appropriate or acceptable ways to meet their needs.

Clear and Explicit Communication

Communicate clearly, concisely, and explicitly. Address behavior issues in the same way.

As previously mentioned, students need you to be clear and explicit. Adding layers of unnecessary niceness to avoid being direct does not do anybody any favors. You need to communicate clearly, concisely, and explicitly. If you are not using a sharp tone or snapping your directions at students, then being direct is not mean nor rude. Many students struggle with complex language and multi-step directions. You therefore should not add additional language to "nice up" your communication. Instead, do that with your tone of voice and your face.

The same rules apply when addressing a behavior: Be clear and explicit. The student is likely elevated/agitated (and you may be also), making clear and explicit communication even more important. And add calm to that list as well. When addressing behaviors, attempt to remain clear, explicit, and calm.

Consider the following classroom situation:

Gredo is walking around the class, flicking things on other students' desks (distracting the whole class) when he should be reading. You need to direct Gredo to his seat and to his reading. This will be difficult to do if you don't like confrontation. Even though you aren't going to be confrontational, you may assume Gredo is going to be confrontational. Assume that you have already attempted to get closer to Gredo and this has not worked, or you are involved in a guided reading session and can't just get up and walk over to him. (Teachers often use proximity as a non-verbal means of redirecting behavior. In this case, the proximity is a cue for Gredo to return to his seat.) You may be tempted to try to be extra nice about it, saying something like, "Gredo, buddy, the other kids are trying to read. It's really hard for them to read when you are walking around distracting them." Gredo may reply with, "I'm not distracting them. They can read."

You are now in a position where you and Gredo disagree with the definition of distraction. This is not a conversation you want (or need) to be having as you have a guided reading group to return your attention to. And really, this may not be a conversation that you ever need to have. The fact is that students are expected to be silently reading when you are doing guided reading. Stick to the facts. "Gredo, you need to be sitting at your seat, please." Very direct, nothing for him to argue with (especially if you have this expectation posted somewhere). You can decide if you require him to be reading right now or if him sitting and not distracting others is enough for now. If you feel he needs to be reading, you might say something like "Gredo, it's silent reading time. Please sit down and read your book."

This example does not include all the other things that may need to happen for Gredo as it is only used to highlight clear and explicit language. Note that Gredo may be a student who frequently distracts and disrupts others during silent reading time. He may have academic issues with reading that need to be evaluated and addressed and you may need to look at a plan to address his distractions and disruptions. Do not expect Gredo to just sit down and begin reading if this is a recurring issue that is more complex than him simply roaming the classroom on this particular day.

Timing

Timing is an important aspect in dealing with any situation. Regardless of how strong a relationship you may have with a student or how positive your rapport with that student may be, a student will never want to lose face in front of their friends. But making a direct statement to a student in front of their peers is not confrontational. Referring back to the previous classroom situation, saying "Gredo, you need to be sitting at your seat please" is not judgmental. It is not specific to Gredo as it is likely something you would, and have, said to many students. It is not a critique of Gredo as a person, or a student, or a reader. It is a clear and explicit statement directing him to sit down.

What would not be advisable would be to point out to Gredo that this is the ninth time he has been out of his seat, or to ask him why it is that you have to tell him to sit down every single day, or point out how he is distracting everyone else. Statements like these are more about Gredo than about his behavior. Gredo will very likely feel the need to save face. Regardless of how much Gredo likes or respects you, you are not going to win this battle.

Continuing with this example:

> Direct Gredo at this point and save the discussion (if you feel you need to) until a later time when there is no audience. If Gredo challenges you, provide the same direction, again remaining calm. Give him a moment or two to respond; he may be weighing the pros and cons of his decision. If Gredo does not follow your direction, offer him a choice between compliance and consequence. Remain positive and calm when you provide this choice. You may wish to say, "Gredo you can either sit in your seat and read your book, or you can go to the library/resource room/office, etc. to read". If he refuses, do not engage in this battle. Discretely send another student to the office for support and continue your guided reading group.

A situation like this requires collaboration and pre-planning. Resource, administration and/or office staff will need to be on board with this plan as it is dependent on their availability. Also, Gredo may have a BSP, and a protocol like this would likely be outlined/documented there.

Rethinking the Meaning of Fairness

Fair does not mean that something happens in exactly the same way for each and every student.

In a classroom, fair means making sure that everyone has access to learning at their level. Fair means that everyone has opportunities to participate and feel successful. It also means that everyone feels recognized for their accomplishments. But fair does not mean that something happens in exactly the same way for each and every student. Fair does not mean the same, nor does it mean equal.

Consider a basic but obvious example. My children love it when I sweep them up into a big hug and kiss them on the cheek. Would it be appropriate to do the same thing with my students at school? What about a less obvious example: I have been giving out stickers for 15 years and students love them. But do you think that ALL my students love stickers? Likely not. There are probably some who don't really care one way or another about stickers. And there are likely one or two who think the stickers are dumb, but they don't say anything about it.

The bottom line is that you need to be very clear in your understanding of fair. If Suzie loves stickers and she gets one every time she passes a test, is it fair that Alex also gets a sticker when he doesn't like them? Should Alex not get something that he likes? Are you sure that everyone getting a sticker is fair? It is definitely equal, but is it fair? Let's extend this a bit more. Suppose you are going to have a pizza party if everyone in the class passes a math test. Dylan is gluten and lactose intolerant, and he doesn't like pizza. You obviously need to get Dylan something else. It is only fair that he should get to enjoy something as well. What matters here is not so much what he gets, as long he gets something he enjoys as much as the rest enjoy pizza.

Fairness means everyone has what they need to experience success.

Are you starting to see that fair and equal are not the same? So, when Jack sits on the wiggle stool because he has issues controlling his energy levels and the wiggle stool helps him divert his energy and be able to focus, you need to be okay with that. It is not unfair that the others don't get a wiggle stool. They may complain because it looks like something fun that they'd like too, but they do not require it and Jack does. If you decide they should all take turns on it (which *seems* fair), then the rest of the class will still be able to focus and learn each day, while Jack will only be able to focus on the days he has the stool. In this example, everyone having a turn with the stool is actually unfair. We could make the same point with crutches, braces, wheelchairs, adaptive technology, and more. Fairness means everyone has what they need to experience success.

It may seem odd to include a discussion of fairness in the chapter on relationships and respect. But if you are dealing with students with challenging behaviors and you are looking at strategies and supports with an inaccurate understanding of fair, you may buy in to the resentment and "not fairs" of the rest of your class. You may subconsciously, or consciously, feel that the students receiving the supports and strategies are overprivileged. This will have a very negative effect on the way you view that student and, consequently, on your relationship with them.

Personalities and Rapport

No two people are alike. Students will connect with some staff members quicker than with others. This is through no fault of the staff members or the students. We are all different and consequently we relate differently to different people. Trying to act differently to relate to students who you aren't clicking with does not often come across as genuine and can be off-putting. Try to be yourself and to find things you might have in common with the students you don't feel connected to.

Sharing insights into your own life can help you connect and develop rapport with your students. Talking about your interests and the interests of your students can also be helpful. For example, a fun chat about which team is winning in the NHL playoffs can be a great icebreaker and can also help make a connection. Going to students' games and extra-curricular activities can show them that you care, regardless of how well you do or don't get along in the classroom. Figure 4.1 shows some other ways to develop rapport with your students.

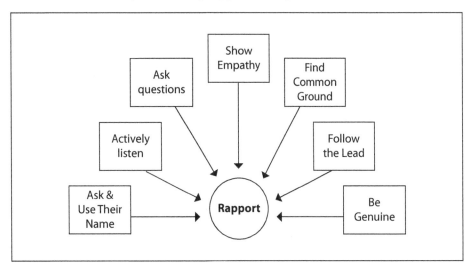

Source: https://m.theindependentbd.com/arcprint/details/67805/2016-11-11

Figure 4.1 Ways to Develop Rapport

Reconsidering Respect

Respect, like rudeness, is something we need to reconsider. Respect is not something that we are owed because we are the educators or the adults. Respect does not work that way, and neither do our students.

Many of us were raised in a generation in which respect was expected, not earned. We respected our elders because they were our elders. It didn't matter what they were like or if they respected us. Our parents would prompt and direct us to be mannerly and respectful, and when we were rude or disrespectful, we were immediately redirected. But society has changed. Today, respect has become more of a two-way street. This is not a judgment on parents; it is merely an observation about societal norms and expectations. We are very much in an era where respect needs to be earned—and rightly so.

A history of negative interactions with adults, caregivers, and even former educators may all be contributing factors to a student's mistrust of authority figures.

Some students with behavior challenges may have a history of negative experiences with adults. Adults in their lives may not have modeled respect, let alone earned it. A history of negative interactions with adults, caregivers, and even former educators may all be contributing factors to a student's mistrust of authority figures. In this context, respect will most definitely need to be earned.

If you subscribe to the theory that underneath every behavior, no matter how challenging or offensive it may be, lies a student in need of support, then you will have no problem earning respect. You will be able to have compassion for the student, while at the same time redirecting the challenging behaviors. When you have a positive relationship with your students, you will come to know them very well. This will be helpful as it will give you insights into why they behave the way they do, and also into things that set them off and the cues that they are becoming agitated.

Repairing Relationships

One of the most important skills you are going to need as you begin addressing challenging behaviors is the ability to repair a relationship after a blow up. It is hard to remain calm and keep your cool during a meltdown or blow up. It can be equally difficult to interact naturally and normally following one. Similarly, it can be awkward, uncomfortable, and even embarrassing for a student to come face to face with you following a blow up or meltdown. Co-regulating this situation can be difficult as both you and the student are in irregular emotional states (see Chapter 5 for more information on co-regulation).

In this situation, you need to mentally move past the behavior. You don't want to rehash the whole thing and it is not useful to be in a place of judgment. Also, as hard as it may be, remember that the situation is not personal and therefore do not respond from a place of personal reaction.

The following provides an example of how to repair a relationship after a meltdown:

> Making an honest statement like, "Hi Ugie, I'm glad you're back," or "Ugie, we're just starting question 4 on page 71" is useful as it invites Ugie back into the classroom and illustrates that you are not harboring any ill feelings. These statements offer the student a clean slate.
>
> Depending on Ugie's needs, she may want a more specific follow up. She may feel badly and want to apologize (but don't take it personally if this is not the case), so don't minimize her need to do this. Make sure to provide a safe place for her to do this. It will be important for you to validate the apology but not to use it as a platform to make things personal. Saying things like, "You wanted to make me feel bad," or "I was shocked that you would say/do that to me" are not useful as they serve to continue feelings of shame and embarrassment. Instead, try saying

statements like, "Thank you for telling me that," or "You know what? I appreciate you sharing that with me. We all have bad days. Today is a new day and I'm just glad you are back." These statements validate what Ugie has said and present a positive place to move forward from.

Rebuilding relationships may be awkward, but it is essential for moving forward. When you are able to repair a relationship, you make that relationship stronger. You and the student have shared a vulnerable moment and have come out of it on a positive note. This may be a new, and much needed, experience for the student. And it is experiences like these that earn respect.

> **TIP** You may find it difficult to rebuild rapport with the student without first addressing the issue at hand. Keep in mind that accountability will happen, just maybe not right away and maybe not in the way you might expect. When having follow-up discussions with the student, make sure that judgments are not part of the conversation. Understanding the situation and expectations, and discussing strategies to prevent a re-occurrence of the issue, should be the focus. Ross Greene's book, *Lost at School*, does a great job illustrating how to navigate this balance with students.

KEY IDEAS

- Relationships and rapport are important aspects of behavior management.
- Remain as emotionally disconnected from behaviors as you can.
- Be clear and explicit with your requests and know you are not being rude.
- Communicate clearly, concisely, and explicitly.
- Making a direct statement to a student in front of their peers is not confrontational when you talk about the behavior.
- Fair does not mean that something happens in exactly the same way for each and every student.
- Sharing insights into your own life and talking about your interests and the interests of your students can help you connect with them.
- Respect needs to be earned.
- It is critical to repair a relationship after a blow up.

5

Self-regulation and Co-regulation

Self-regulation is the ability to monitor and manage emotions and feelings like anger, excitement, frustration, or anxiety.

Self-regulation is the ability to monitor and manage emotions and feelings like anger, excitement, frustration, or anxiety. It is probably the most common goal for students who present with challenging behaviors. We want students to be aware of their emotions and emotional responses, and to manage them in a positive and successful way. This is a BIG goal. Self-regulation skills can take years for a student to acquire, and the process usually begins in infancy.

Helping students monitor and regulate their strong emotions through positive and continued interactions is referred to as co-regulation. Co-regulation is defined as "warm and responsive interactions that provide the support, coaching, and modeling children need to understand, express, and modulate their thoughts, feeling, and behaviors" (Murray et al., 2015, 14). In addition, co-regulation "requires teachers and providers to pay close attention to the cues students send and respond consistently and sensitively over time with just the right amount of support" (Gillespie, Zero to Three, https://www.zerotothree.org/resources/1777-it-takes-two-the-role-of-co-regulation-in-building-self-regulation-skills).

Developing Self-regulation Skills

Self-soothing in infancy develops into self-regulation as the child grows older.

Jody Carrington, child psychologist, refers to students who are in the midst of a behavioral or emotional meltdown as having "flipped their lids." She describes this type of behavior as very normal behavior that stems back to infancy. Typically, when infants "flip their lids" their caregivers meet their needs, over and over and over (i.e., feeding, changing their diaper, snuggling, soothing talk, etc.). These repeated acts of caring, over time, provide the infant with the skills they need to begin to self-sooth. Self-soothing in infancy develops into self-regulation as the child grows older.

Some students, for a variety of reasons, do not develop the skills they need to put their lids back on. The good news is that even though students may come to school unable to self-regulate, you can help them develop these essential skills.

And it is never too late to learn these skills. Think back to infants and the number of times they are supported in putting their lid back on. Nurturing self-regulation is a slow process accomplished through the repeated process of supporting a student when they have "flipped their lid."

Helping a student to put their lid back on while maintaining a calm, positive, and compassionate approach is co-regulation. There are three aspects to co-regulation (https://fpg.unc.edu/sites/fpg.unc.edu/files/resources/reports-and-policy-briefs/Co-RegulationFromBirthThroughYoungAdulthood.pdf):

- **Provide a warm, responsive relationship** – Show an interest in students' lives, show that you care, and respond to their needs and wants.
- **Structure the environment** – Create a physically and emotionally safe environment for students with consistent routines and expectations.
- **Teach/coach self-regulation skills** – Use modeling, instruction, practice, and reinforcement so students develop successful self-regulation skills.

The process of co-regulation may become frustrating over time as you may feel like you have put a student's lid on a million times and are no further ahead. This is not the case. Each time you support a student in this way, you have made progress. It is just sometimes hard to see when you are at the centre of it.

In this situation, data collection may help highlight progress that may not be obvious otherwise. Data collection may reveal that the student is having fewer meltdowns, that the meltdowns are less intense, or that the duration of the meltdowns is decreasing. It may also be that the meltdowns are resulting in less severe consequences, such as the student being able to return to class versus having to be sent home. Progress can take many forms when dealing with behavior. (See Chapter 7 for more information on data collection.)

The purpose of co-regulation is to develop self-regulation skills in students.

The purpose of co-regulation is to develop self-regulation skills in students. Some of the strategies you use to help students calm down to prevent a meltdown or recover after a meltdown (de-escalation) may be things they can eventually use independently. The student may become more able to identify when a meltdown is coming on and then use these strategies proactively to prevent it from happening. As the student's self-regulation begins to develop, you may find yourself cuing the student more (e.g., How are you doing? Do you need a break? You seem upset, what do you need? Why don't you try your breathing? This may be a good time for you to go for a walk., etc.) and providing less support for meltdowns. This is a great step toward self-regulation. You still have an important role in the process, but it is a definite step in the right direction.

The Importance of Co-regulation

Co-regulation is, by far, the most valuable skill you can possess and demonstrate as a teacher.

Co-regulation is, by far, the most valuable skill you can possess and demonstrate as a teacher. Research currently stresses the importance of co-regulation for students learning to self-regulate their emotions:

> Neuroscience shows that humans develop their abilities for emotional self-regulation through connections with reliable caregivers who soothe and model in a process called "co-regulation." Since many troubled young people have not experienced a reliable, comforting presence, they have difficulty regulating their emotions and impulses. Co-regulation provides a practical model for helping young people learn to manage immediate emotions and develop long term self-control.

(Michael McKnight, Paces in Education, https://www.pacesconnection.com/g/aces-in-education/blog/co-regulation-with-students-at-risk-calming-together)

It is also important to note that when you are engaged in co-regulation with a student, you are also co-regulating for the rest of your class. Consider the following classroom situation involving Levi, a student who could be described as a silent bully (i.e., always flying under the radar, never saying or doing anything when adults are around):

> The other students are very intimidated by Levi. The teacher and support staff struggle to engage Levi in any meaningful way and complaints about him have continued to pile up throughout the year. The staff have implemented countless strategies and supports for Levi but are not seeing any gains academically, behaviorally, or socially. The support staff are considering alternate educational opportunities for him.
>
> Although they feel they are starting to get through to him in terms of building a relationship, they are concerned for the other students in the class. They are worried that being in a constant state of fear or intimidation will have a negative impact on the students both academically and emotionally. The staff feel like they are being pulled in two very different directions—acting in Levi's best interest or acting in the best interest of the rest of the class.
>
> The staff decides to facilitate a meeting with the multiple support persons involved in Levi's programming and share their concerns. The psychologist points out that each time he demonstrates intimidating and explosive behavior and the teacher and support staff respond in a safe and caring manner, they are co-regulating for all the students in the class. The staff had never thought about co-regulation in that way before.
>
> This is a game changer for the staff. They are no longer consumed by what had initially seemed like competing best interests (those of Levi and those of the rest of the class) and are now able to continue to address Levi's behaviors with the lens of co-regulating for the rest of the class. This realization is not only liberating for the staff, it also gives them a feeling of connectedness with the other students in relation to Levi's behaviors.

Co-regulating with the Audience

As discussed above, it is important not to forget the rest of the students in the class, those who witness explosive behaviors that may make them scared or uncomfortable. The approaches described in this chapter can support these students in learning the skills to deal with many kinds of uncomfortable situations, such as in school, in relationships, in social settings, and in the workplace. The ability to work through discomfort is a good skill for students to develop.

But for students who have a history of behavior issues, you have a team of people at your school who are, or can be, involved in providing support to you, your student, and the rest of your class.

When thinking about students who have meltdowns, remember you are not alone. You may have a student who, due to a combination of factors (e.g., their dog died, their parents are separating, their grandparent died, they failed a test, etc.), has an unanticipated meltdown. This may be a one-time thing given the circumstances rather than the beginning of a behavioral pattern, which you can handle in the moment. But for students who have a history of behavior issues, you have a team of people at your school who are, or can be, involved in providing support to you, your student, and the rest of your class.

Another important thing to remember, which we referred to earlier, is that when students are confronted in front of their peers, they will usually try to save face before any other type of response. This is why removing the student, or removing the audience, is usually a key part of behavior plans. You will not make headway with a student who feels their responses are under the scrutiny of their peers.

Maintaining Emotional Detachment

As mentioned in Chapter 1, it is important to remain emotionally disconnected from behaviors as much as possible. Students are not doing these behaviors *to you* or *at you*. This is much easier said than done, but it is essential when considering co-regulation.

It is impossible to model appropriate responses when you are drawn into the battle. And unfortunately, when a student is experiencing escalated emotions, they may purposely engage in behaviors to draw you in, and you are likely in a state of lessened patience and heightened frustrations. During these times, the student may use statements to engage you in dialogue, such as "I hate myself," "I wish I was dead," "You don't like me," "You just want me to fail," or "You don't even care." Don't feel badly if you have been drawn in by such statements. Although you may want to clarify or rectify these things, it is important to keep in mind that this is not the time and these conversations only serve to detract from the issues and behaviors at hand.

> **TIP** Co-regulation is not easy, especially if you are emotionally invested in the situation. Falling prey to a power-struggle with a student exhibiting problematic behavior is counter-productive in terms of co-regulation.

Factors Associated with Co-regulation

The National Institute for Children's Health Quality (NICHQ) has created an acronym, AGILE, to help parents remember the important factors of co-regulation. Although it was created for parents, the approach and acronym may also be useful for educators.

The AGILE approach to co-regulating responses advises parents/educators to pay close attention to the following (NICHQ, https://www.nichq.org/insight/childrens-social-and-emotional-development-starts-co-regulation):

- **A – Affect**: Your tone and expressions show your emotions. In times of stress, ensure that your affect is supportive and soothing.
- **G – Gesture**: Facial expressions, hand gestures, body movement, posturing, and pacing all reflect your emotions and are felt by a student during your interactions.
- **I – Intonation**: Modulating the tone of your voice helps conveys affect and social/emotional meaning. This is "felt" and "understood" long before words. And even after language develops, affect, gestures, and intonation convey the genuine meaning of the interpersonal exchange. This communication is stronger than words.
- **L – Latency (Wait)**: Wait and give the student time to take in your gestures and intonations. Co-regulation requires patience.

It is impossible to model appropriate responses when you are drawn into the battle.

- **E – Engagement**: Before you continue, be sure you have engaged the student. The student's facial expressions, words, and body language will tell you if they are engaged.

See the Recommended Resources section at the end of the book for more information about emotional regulation.

> **TIP** We are not born with co-regulation skills. It takes time and practice to be able to co-regulate, especially in the face of more explosive behaviors. Once we learn not to engage in the battle, we are better able to navigate the behavior for the student who is having the issue as well as any who are witnessing the behavior. As teachers, we set the tone.

KEY IDEAS

- Self-regulation is the ability to monitor and manage emotions and feelings like anger, excitement, frustration, or anxiety.
- Co-regulation is helping students monitor and regulate their strong emotions through positive and continued interactions.
- Even though students may come to school unable to self-regulate, you can help them develop these essential skills.
- The purpose of co-regulation is to develop self-regulation skills in students.
- When you are engaged in co-regulation with a student, you are also co-regulating for the rest of your class.
- Remain as emotionally disconnected from behaviors as possible.
- The AGILE approach to co-regulating responses advises parents/educators to pay close attention to affect, gesture, intonation, latency, and engagement.

6

Reinforcement

Reinforcement is the process by which you increase a specific behavior. In the simplest of terms, you observe a desired behavior, you reinforce that behavior, and that behavior occurs more often. One of the key factors in reinforcement is using things that you know are motivating (reinforcing) to the student. What you offer as reinforcement *must* be more reinforcing than what the student is currently getting out of the misbehavior.

For example, if a student misbehaves to get sent out of class, you need to offer the student something that is more motivating than getting out of class. You may also choose to offer "getting out of class" as the reinforcement since you know the student is motivated by this. However, for this to work you must ensure that the student is no longer removed from class for misbehavior and instead only gets out of class as a reinforcement for appropriate behavior.

Choosing Reinforcers

A variety of preference and choice surveys are available online to help you determine what may be reinforcing to a student.

A variety of preference and choice surveys are available online to help you determine what may be reinforcing to a student. You may also know the student's interests well enough to determine what might be reinforcing to them. Try asking the student's parents for ideas or have a conversation with the student, depending on their ability to discuss such things. Regardless of how you determine what will work as a reinforcer, the important thing is that you are sure the student will be motivated to access/acquire it.

Reinforcers don't have to be tangible; instead, they can be activities that the student enjoys. Table 5.1 (on the next page) provides some examples of reinforcers depending on the age and developmental level of the student.

Table 6.1: Examples of Reinforcers

Primary	Elementary	Junior High	High School
• Blowing bubbles • Listening to music • Water play • Sand play • Sensory activities (e.g., rocking on the rocking chair, bouncing on a trampoline) • Listening to a story being read aloud • Playing with a favorite toy • Watching a video • Building a puzzle • Coloring • Stacking blocks • Reading with a partner • Playing a game with a friend • Extra outside time • Going to the gym	• Time on technology • Playing a game with a peer • Gym time with friends • Helping the custodian • Free time • Playing a game with a staff member • Sharing a piece of work with a staff member • Art activity • Craft activity • Earning a lunchtime video for the class • Earning an extra recess for the class • Choosing the gym sport for the day/week	• Time on technology • Free time • Extra time in the library • Time for a special project, such as painting, building a model, working on a puzzle • Reading comics with a friend • Choosing a friend and helping set up for a special activity (e.g., assembly, concert) • Sharing a morning announcement (e.g., weather forecast, upcoming special event) • Earning the opportunity to be picked up from school versus taking the bus	• Time on technology • Free time • Free time with a peer • Time for a special project, such as painting, building a model, or working on a puzzle, a robotics project, or a technology project • Challenging a staff member to a game of chess, cribbage, etc. • Extra gym time (or extra time in the weight room) • A class pass • Wearing the mascot uniform at a school game • Helping the coach at a practice or game

This list is by no means exhaustive. The important thing is that the activity is something the student will be motivated to do. See the Recommended Resources section at the end of the book for examples of preference surveys.

Once you figure out the motivation piece, you need to be sure that the student does not become "bored" with the reinforcer. One way to combat this is to offer the student a choice. If you have identified several reinforcers, offer the student a choice of what they are working toward. If they pick the same video 17 times in a row, so be it; they are obviously motivated to watch it if they are choosing it. By offering the student a choice, they are less likely to grow tired of the reinforcers. If they express a disinterest, ask them what else might work. If it is doable, add it to the list!

Some reinforcers are not appropriate. For example, it would not be possible to watch a full-length movie every time you want to reinforce a behavior. Also, some reinforcers in Table 6.1 may not be possible in your environment (e.g., a class pass or getting picked up versus taking the bus). These would need to be approved in advance. Parents/guardians would need to be on board with a school pick up, teachers and administrators would need to be okay with the idea of a class pass—and they would have conditions regarding frequency, duration, etc.

Another way to help ensure that reinforcers do not lose their motivational impact is to not allow the student to access the reinforcer in any other way or at any other time. For instance, why would a student do three pages of math to watch their favorite videos if they have access to videos during their breaks? The student could refuse to do their math and then watch their videos at the next break.

Try offering the student a choice of what reinforcer they are working toward.

Pairing friends/peers with reinforcement can be a great way to help develop and support positive relationships.

Some of the reinforcers included in Table 5.1 refer to friends. Students who have behavior issues often struggle with positive relationships. Pairing friends/peers with reinforcement can be a great way to help develop and support positive relationships. It can also act as additional motivation if the student likes peer attention and/or is motivated by peer interactions. When you add a peer to the mix, it is important to make sure you have the appropriate permissions. You may need to seek permission/approval from the peer's teacher, administration, and even the peer's parent/guardian depending on the context (e.g., how often the peer is involved, what class the peer may be missing time from, how often this is occurring, the duration of the event, etc.).

Another thing you need to look at when thinking about reinforcement is whether the reinforcer matches your expectations. Make sure that your expectations and the reinforcement align in value. With reinforcement, start off by tipping the balance to over-valuing the expectations. Consider the following example:

> Initially Nat isn't doing any work in math class. Begin by offering him two minutes with his favorite book for each problem he completes. This may seem inappropriate because there is too much time off-task with this schedule of reinforcement. But remember that you are starting at a point where Nat isn't doing any math. With this schedule of reinforcement, he will go from not being at all productive to producing some work. As Nat gets comfortable with the reinforcement system, gradually increase his expectations.

Not all educators are comfortable with reinforcement, at least not at first. You may feel that you are bribing students to behave. Instead, try thinking about it as reinforcing positive, appropriate, and desired behavior. The student performs the behavior, and you offer a reinforcement. In contrast, bribery involves giving the desired item in advance and then expecting (sometimes pleading with) the student to comply with their end of the deal.

Some educators also express concerns that reinforcement systems are unfair as students who always behave aren't getting anything. In reality, the students who always behave are in fact getting a lot of reinforcement, you just may not see it. These students are motivated in more natural ways, such as by your smiles, your looks of approval, your comments (written and verbal), praise, and more. Some of these students are also motivated by other natural means, such as outperforming a peer or beating a previous score.

Students who require a reinforcement system often do not obtain reinforcement through these natural means. Providing more obvious and targeted reinforcement is leveling the playing field for them. And it also provides you with a means of building their responsiveness to those natural means of reinforcement. When you provide a student with a reinforcer, it is imperative that you pair it with natural reinforcement.

For example:

> When giving Vozwol his Mario sticker, smile, maybe pat his shoulder, and say something very positive and explicit about his behavior (the behavior that earned him the sticker), such as "Great job raising your hand Vozwol! I like how you waited for me to call your name." Eventually Vozwol will respond to your smiles, your tone of voice, and your pats on the shoulder in the same way as he would to the stickers. But this will take time.

Starting a Reinforcement Program

When starting a reinforcement program, go overboard by offering the reinforcement as often as you can to get the student to buy in. For instance:

> Sally never stays in her seat for more than 30 seconds. Begin by offering her reinforcement every 20 seconds. Choosing 20 seconds serves a very significant purpose: It ensures that Sally will be successful. If you had decided to reinforce Sally if she sat in her seat for 60 seconds, she may have never met that goal and therefore would never get her reinforcer and not be motivated to stay in her seat. (See Chapter 7 on data collection for ideas on how to choose appropriate starting points.)

You may be concerned about having the time to offer reinforcement every 20 seconds—it can seem very overwhelming. If you are at a point where Sally can't stay in her seat for 30 seconds, you probably have other supports and/or services in place for her. Perhaps she has an educational assistant (EA) or receives support from a resource teacher. She may see a counselor or be on the radar with administration. Regardless, if you are starting her off with an interval of every 20 seconds, you will need some help facilitating that for the first little while. If you can do this consistently from the onset, you can quickly move past the 20 second mark to a place where you are able to manage the intervals without support. Also, depending on Sally's abilities, she may be able to self-monitor her intervals with a timer—you and your school team would need to gauge the appropriateness of this. (See Chapter 10 for more information about using timers.)

Reinforcement needs to happen immediately *following the positive behavior.*

Reinforcement needs to happen *immediately* following the positive behavior. Consider the following classroom example:

> Your goal for Marco is that he raise his hand instead of blurting out. As soon as Marco does this, you need to reinforce him. If he has an EA or other form of support worker, they can quietly praise his efforts and offer him reinforcement as soon as he raises his hand. Or, you can call on Marco as soon as you get the chance. You can also acknowledge him immediately by saying something like, "Marco I see you have your hand up, good for you! As soon as Todd is finished, I will call on you next." Or "Marco thank you for raising your hand! I'll answer your question in just a minute."

When a student regularly demonstrates success, you need to increase the expectations. This consequently fades the reinforcement schedule, meaning the student will be expected to do increasingly more work before receiving reinforcement, which is what you want. The goal is to move from a reinforcement system that is occurring frequently throughout the day, to something that could be weekly or even monthly depending on the size of the reinforcement and the ability of the student to wait that long.

Immediate versus Delayed Reinforcement

Students need reinforcement immediately following the desired behavior, otherwise you may be unintentionally reinforcing a negative behavior, as shown in the following example:

> Alex is being reinforced for telling his peers to "stop" rather than hitting. Alex tells Hameed to stop. You overhear this and make a mental note that you need to reinforce him. You get caught up in a question another student asks, and it takes a couple of minutes to get to Alex. When you do, he is crawling around on the floor under his desk. This is not something you want to encourage. However, if you give him his reinforcer at this point (because you still owe him one for the "stop" a couple of minutes ago), you may be reinforcing this behavior regardless of any verbal reference to why you are giving him the reinforcer.

In this situation, you may need to look at immediate versus delayed reinforcement. Receiving a Smartie, a sticker, a chance to blow bubbles, or something else as soon as the desired behavior occurs is immediate reinforcement. Earning an extra recess later in the afternoon or a class movie on Friday is delayed reinforcement.

Many students are not at a point where they can wait for delayed reinforcement. This is unfortunate as you can often offer larger, more motivating options if you can delay them. Although you can't offer a two-hour movie every time a student raises their hand, what if there was a way to offer a movie if the student raises their hand all week or a certain number of times? It would be much more feasible to show a movie once a month, as opposed to daily. What you need is a way to offer immediate reinforcement toward a delayed reinforcer. Token systems are great for this.

Token Systems of Reinforcement

With a token system of reinforcement, the student earns a token immediately following the desired behavior, but the actual reinforcer happens later.

With a token system of reinforcement, the student earns a token (such as a bingo stamp on a chart, a marble, a ticket, a sticker, or something else) immediately following the desired behavior, but the actual reinforcer happens later. Token systems can be complex, and it is important to make sure that the student is able to hold out for delayed reinforcement. You can also give the student a choice in this. Perhaps the student can choose something immediate or choose to earn a token/ticket/something else toward the bigger, but delayed, reinforcement. There is no one right way to do this. As long as the reinforcement works for you and works for the student, then you are on the right track.

Once the student is experiencing success on a regular basis, consider pulling back the reinforcement. In a primary or an elementary setting, for example, you may go from reinforcing multiple times throughout the day to providing reinforcement before recess, before lunch, and at the end of the day. In this way, the reinforcement system fades.

A Note of Caution about Token Systems

When a student is earning tokens toward a reinforcer, be careful not to get caught in the trap of "in a row."

When a student is earning tokens toward a reinforcer, be careful not to get caught in the trap of "in a row." You may think about offering reinforcement depending on a set number of appropriate behaviors in a row. For instance, if a student gets a green in all three of his day blocks, they can go outside for the last 20 minutes of the day. Similarly, if a student has four good days in a row, they can make a model car during lunch break.

You may do this for several reasons. First, you very likely believe that students can maintain good behavior for these amounts of time. Second, it would work well for you if you were able to motivate students for longer periods of time. And, lastly, it seems like a logical move in fading reinforcement, as we discussed above.

The student may over-focus on the reinforcer or on their behavior and may unintentionally behave in a less than favorable manner.

The downside with "in a row" is that you may be setting yourself and your student up for failure. Generally, when you offer "in a row" reinforcement, the reinforcer is very desirable to the student, more so than the things the student may work toward throughout any given day. Sometimes the pressure of this highly motivating object/activity can be counterintuitive. The student may over-focus on the reinforcer or on their behavior and may unintentionally behave in a less than favorable manner.

Consider the following example of a student, Anand, who has been having great success with his reinforcement program:

> Things have been going well, communication between home and school is very positive, and reports from home suggest that the parents are pleased with the progress as well. One morning you are called to the bus because Anand will not come into the school. When you board the bus, Anand is crying in the front seat. He has his head in his hands and is talking to himself through choked off sobs. "I can't have a bad day" he sobs, "I just can't. Mom said if I have a bad day I can't go to the store for a treat after school."
>
> Anand is overwhelmed by this level of pressure. His mom has been so pleased with his behavior, both at home and at school, that she is using taking him to the store after school as a reward for having such good days. The student has internalized this to mean that if he steps out of line even once during the day, his trip to the store will be cancelled. This level of perceived pressure is too much for him. "In a row" offers can often have the same effect.

This is very similar to the student who continuously parrots, "but can I still play cars with Mr. C?" every time he is spoken to. The focus on the reinforcement and the pressure of not losing that reinforcement can take away the student's focus from the task at hand. This can get frustrating, and you may start to say things like "We'll see," or "It depends on how much work you get done." These comments, though well-intentioned, suggest to the student that playing cars with Mr. C may not be happening today. This could increase the student's stress or anxiety and add another layer to their lack of focus and productivity.

Below is an example of the "in a row" contingency and the issues that can accompany this:

> Stephanie gets to work on her model if she has four good days in a row. Let's say she has had three great days in a row. Last night her older sister didn't come home, and her family was awake worried most of the night, so her day didn't start like it typically would. You can assume that Stephanie may not have a great morning. If Stephanie feels like she has blown her chance on the fourth good day, that may set her off for the rest of the day. There will be no point in Stephanie trying to get herself back on track at all today as the "in a row" would mean she will be starting back at zero on the next school day and will have lost any value from the three great days she just had.

The same philosophy exists for "in a row" offers through the day (or whole day offers). In this case, if they experience an issue at any point in the day, that becomes compounded by their frustration with having lost the opportunity for reinforcement at the end of the day. This can often lead to increased problem behavior and provides little motivation for the student to get their behavior back on track. This can be hard for everyone involved.

On the flip side, if you have been on an "in a row" or whole day schedule and something happens (e.g., such as the student whose sister didn't come home), you may feel compelled to change the rules for this situation. Empathy and compassion may suggest that it is unfair to penalize the student for a situation that is outside of their control and very obviously upsetting. And if the student did pull their day around in the face of this situation, you would be really motivated to reinforce them for that. And rightly so. The downfall is that changing the rules for reinforcement may give the student the false impression that they can negotiate reinforcement—and this is not something you want to promote.

Instead, the best thing to do would be to offer the student reinforcement as soon as they get themselves back on track, but with a different reinforcer. Don't change the reinforcement program you have set up (e.g., working on a model after appropriate behavior for four days in a row). When you offer the reinforcement, be very explicit about how proud you are of the student for turning their day around. Offer them something highly preferred as this level of regulation is exactly the behavior you are trying to develop. You could even offer the student a choice between a few highly preferred reinforcers or ask them what they would like.

You could then at some point in the day discuss the "in a row" reinforcement system with the student. Tell them that although you know they can achieve this, you realize that it may not account for unforeseen things that come up (e.g., her sister not coming home) and therefore may not be fair. Discuss alternatives and explain the process of accumulating days using student friendly language. If you and the student both agree to this, Stephanie, the student in our example, would only need to have one more great day to begin working on her model. This is a win and a success for everyone. This approach allows you to move away from the "in a row" approach and it is less likely that student will think they can negotiate

The downfall is that changing the rules for reinforcement may give the student the false impression that they can negotiate reinforcement—and this is not something you want to promote.

or change the reinforcement schedule as it was you who broached the subject after the student had received reinforcement for turning things around.

When you offer reinforcement on a cumulative basis, such as a reinforcer once a student earns five tokens, it gives the student an immediate reason to get their behavior back on track after an incident. You may actually be able to use their cumulative status as motivation for them to get back on track. Think back to Stephanie. Imagine if you were able to say, "You know what Stephanie, we had a rough morning. You have a lot going on. Let's focus on getting you back on track today so you can earn that model time tomorrow!"

You want students to learn that there are consequences to behavior—good and bad.

You want students to learn that there are consequences to behavior—good and bad. What you don't want them to learn is that good behavior can be for naught, that one bad moment can erase a bank of good ones, or that negative behavior holds more value than positive behavior. "In a row" offers can promote these ideas. Reinforcement should be a positive experience and needs to promote and value successes over failures.

Subject-specific Reinforcement

Students often have difficulty with specific tasks or subjects. For example, students with ASD often find gym and music particularly difficult. This is due to many factors, including sensory overstimulation due to sounds, echoes, volume, and more. Some students have difficulty just entering the classroom due to sensory overload, let alone participating in the class. In this situation, you may have to begin by working toward getting the student into the room, and then focus on participating. Consider the following example of Devin, a student with ASD:

> Depending on the severity of Devin's needs, try offering reinforcement just for touching the door, eventually moving to standing at the door for a brief period of time, standing inside the door for an increasing amount of time, sitting in a seat or at a desk just inside the door for increasing amounts of time, participating for a short duration of time, and then participating for increasing amounts of time. This can take anywhere from days, to weeks, to months, depending on your starting point.

You may also have a student who starts off strong but isn't able to maintain focus for the full duration of the period. For instance:

> Offer reinforcement for a successful amount of time, and gradually grow that to the full length of time. Or, conversely, bring Devin to class after it has started so he is only there for a short (yet successful) amount of time and reinforce successful completion of class. Gradually bring him earlier and earlier until he is participating for the full duration. Also consider ways Devin could earn tokens for successfully participating in tasks during class, giving him the ability to leave class once he has earned a set number of tokens.

Try to start as simple as possible, and only make the system more complex if simple doesn't work.

There is no limit to how you can reinforce behavior. Just remember, the simpler the system of reinforcement, the easier it will be to fade later on. Try to start as simple as possible, and only make the system more complex if simple doesn't work.

The Important Features of Reinforcement

The acronym DISC is used in many behavior programs and resources. It outlines the important features of reinforcement that you need to remember.

- **D – Desirability (or Deprivation):** Reinforcers must be something the student wants. Remember just because you *think* they would like/want it, doesn't mean they will. You also need to ensure the student does not become saturated with their reinforcer (i.e., they get it so often as a reinforcer that it loses its motivational value).
- **I – Immediacy:** Reinforcement must happen *immediately* following the target behavior. If you are earning something for later (e.g., a movie at the end of the month), make sure the checkmark or token is given immediately following the desired behavior.
- **S – Size:** The size of the reinforcer must equal the size of the expectation. If you are offering one token for one multiplication problem, you can't expect the student to complete their multiplication quiz for one token.
- **C – Contingent:** Make sure the reinforcer is contingent on the behavior. In other words, the behavior must happen in order for the student to access the reinforcer. The student should not have access to the reinforcer outside of the reinforcement system.

Reinforcement versus Punishment

Reinforcement is a process that increases a behavior; punishment decreases a behavior.

By definition, reinforcement is a process that increases a behavior, while punishment decreases a behavior. Punishment sometimes feels like it works instantly, and on the surface, it doesn't seem to require as much time or effort as reinforcement. For instance, you raise your voice, maybe even yell, and things quiet down. Raising your voice or yelling are punishers in this example as they decrease the behaviors that had been occurring.

So why go to all the bother of reinforcement? There are several reasons. Reinforcement:
- builds replacement behaviors;
- builds appropriate behaviors;
- lasts over time;
- can be paired with natural reinforcement to level the playing field; and
- is positive and helps build relationships and respect.

In contrast, punishment:
- does not build replacement behaviors;

- does not build appropriate behaviors;
- can be detrimental;
- does not promote respect;
- can be embarrassing for the student and cause them to shut down or feel isolated/exposed; and
- can sometimes hit a little too close to home for some of students (e.g., although yelling may settle a student who is struggling, yelling may also be a consequence they experience at home and could be paired with other negative forms of punishment).

As easy as it may sometimes be to punish, we encourage you to reinforce positive behaviors as often as you can.

As easy as it may sometimes be to punish, we encourage you to reinforce positive behaviors as often as you can.

KEY IDEAS

- Reinforcement is the process by which you increase a specific behavior.
- A variety of preference and choice surveys are available online to help you determine what may be reinforcing to a student. (See the Recommended Resources section at the end of the book for examples.)
- Reinforcers can be tangible or they can be activities that the student enjoys.
- By offering the student a choice, they are less likely to grow tired of the reinforcers.
- When you provide a student with a reinforcer, you need to pair it with natural reinforcement.
- When starting a reinforcement program, go overboard by offering the reinforcement as often as you can.
- Reinforcement needs to happen *immediately* following the positive behavior.
- When a student demonstrates success regularly, increase the expectations.
- Consider the effectiveness of immediate versus delayed reinforcement for the student.
- With a token system of reinforcement, the student earns a token immediately following the desired behavior, but the actual reinforcer happens later.
- When using a token system, be careful not to get caught in the trap of "in a row."
- Subject-specific reinforcement is effective for students who have difficulty with specific tasks or subjects.
- The important features of reinforcement are desirability, immediacy, size, and contingent.
- Reinforcement is a process that increases a behavior; punishment decreases a behavior.

7

....

Data Collection

Make the collection process as simple as possible.

Although data is often the most useful tool in addressing challenging behavior, it is also the most underused. Dealing with challenging behavior can be very draining and can take up a considerable amount of time. It is not surprising that the thought of collecting data seems overwhelming.

Make the collection process as simple as possible. The person collecting the data should not need to take five minutes each time a behavior occurs to write down a word-for-word account of everything they watched unfold. Nobody has time for this, and it is not an optimal use of time. Using a checklist to collect data can be very useful for all parties involved. You can find a wide variety of data collection checklists online. (See the Recommended Resources section at the end of the book for examples of templates.)

> **TIP** Depending on the behavior(s) you are monitoring, you may be able to seek support. We frequently reference the school team as a primary support when dealing with challenging behavior. If you have the involvement of the school team, a resource teacher, or a classroom EA, you may be able to delegate the data collection process. Although EAs often collect data, keep in mind that EAs can also feel overwhelmed by the behaviors, especially if they are assigned to work with/support the student.

Guidelines for Data Collection

The location of the data records, the timing of the data collection, and the accuracy of the data collected are all important aspects to consider.

Location

Easy accessibility and privacy/confidentiality are the two main factors to consider when choosing where to store the data collection forms.

The location of the data records may or may not be an important consideration depending on the context of your class and the number of people involved with the student. Easy accessibility and privacy/confidentiality are the two main factors to consider when choosing where to store the data collection forms. Although you want to ensure student privacy/confidentiality, the records must also be easily accessible by all staff who are using them. As a result, a filing cabinet or a teacher planning book may not be optimal locations.

You may wish to put the data in a folder so the information is private, but then leave the folder in a specified location. The location is sometimes self-determined. If you are keeping data on how often a student is sent to a time-out area, for example, then it only makes sense to keep the data records in or by that area. The staff member involved can complete the data record while the student is calming down. Any staff member who is supporting the student with the time-out can follow this process.

> **TIP** Different jurisdictions may have specific guidelines around time-out locations and corresponding data collection. Consult with your school's administrator or resource teacher to make sure you are following any established protocols. This may also be the case if your school has a sensory room.

When data collection is not linked to a specific location, other considerations come into play. For example, if EAs are sharing work with more challenging students to prevent burn-out, consider the easiest way for the EAs to share and access data collection records. It is often not optimal for each EA to have their own data collection records. It can be useful for the EAs to gain a perspective of the student's whole day, so being able to see the data from other points in the day can be helpful. It is also easier to chart and analyze data from one set of records than from multiple sets.

You also don't want to create an atmosphere of success and failure between staff members, with one staff member not experiencing much challenging behavior and another having multiple issues each time they interact with the student. There are many possible reasons why one staff member may appear to have more success than another. For example:

- The student may have a better rapport with one staff member than another.
- The student may have a particular dislike for the subject(s) that one staff member is always there for.
- One staff member may always be assigned to the transition times (coming in from recess/lunch, etc.), which the student has difficulty with.

Not sharing data is not going to make these differences any less of a reality, it just may help keep it from being blatantly obvious. And if this is the case, you can look at the data to identify why this may be the case to help the staff member understand that this is not personal.

Despite these considerations, you may still choose to have staff members collect their own data. If it makes sense for your situation, given these considerations, then go with that process.

Timing

It is also important to consider when the data is being collected. It will not be possible to record the aspects of the behavior while it is occurring. And it may not be possible to do this until much later in the day, depending on who is collecting the data. The greater the amount of time between the behavior and the recording, the less accurate it may be.

Identify who will be recording the data, and look at when, realistically, this can be done. The simpler you can make the recording template, the more possible it may be for a staff member to fill it in as immediately as possible following the behavior episode. Data collection checklists can help simplify data collection, making it easier to complete in a short amount of time. The teacher, or other involved staff members, may wish to make a more detailed report for their own records when they have more time.

Accuracy

Checklist templates help keep the data collection more factual. When a student has had a meltdown, you or other staff members may understandably be very frustrated or upset by the behavior. But completing a data collection chart in the midst of your own emotional stresses can sometimes lead to inaccurate reporting.

You want an informed report of what happened, why it happened, the time it happened, how long it lasted (possibly), and any resulting consequences. Other data may be required, but this too should be recorded and reported factually. When charting the data to look for patterns, the accuracy of the data is very important as it will be the basis for measuring progress and determining the need for revising any plans/strategies in place.

Collecting Baseline Data

When student behaviors and challenges are overwhelming, you may start to feel like these things are happening all the time. You may also feel like the behaviors happen for no reason, or that the student is melting down over everything. You may feel this especially if you have been trying to manage these challenges and behaviors for a long period of time.

The good news is that things are often not as bad as they seem. Baseline data is data you collect before you put any strategies in place. Collect a solid chunk of data, such as over a week or two, and then analyze it for patterns. You will use these patterns to develop strategies and suggestions or build a behavior support plan. Baseline data provides a look at the behavior at its worst before you have intervened. It gives you a bar from which to measure the success of your intervention. Just seeing that the behavior is not occurring all the time or is occurring for a particular reason provides a feeling of manageability.

> **TIP** Baseline data offers you a different view of things and may help you feel that things are not quite as bad as you initially thought.

A team member often analyzes baseline data and then reviews it with the teacher and the rest of the team. Fresh eyes and multiple perspectives offer more options for how to proceed. It also helps you know that you are not alone and that you have a whole team supporting the student and the behavior. This can be very reassuring.

Types of Data

Before you start collecting data, consider what it is you want to know and/or track about the behavior. Important things to collect might include:
- the specific behavior(s) that occurred;
- the time the behavior occurred; and
- the initials of the staff member collecting the data.

These things are pretty quick to jot down and won't be overly taxing in terms of time or effort. They will also lend themselves nicely to pattern identification. You can use the time the behavior occurred to determine what was going on (e.g., 10:05 is when students were going outside). This eliminates having to write that down. Again, try to keep things as simple as possible.

You still need to look at what it is you want to track. If you want to know how often a behavior happens, look at frequency. If you want to know how long a behavior lasts, you need a way to track duration. Frequency data is usually the most common type of data collected. However, some very useful insights can come out of duration tracking.

For example, consider the following example of the importance of duration tracking:

> Ana, who often hides in a corner and sobs. You start by tracking how often this behavior happens and determine that it happens multiple times a day and seems to be related to demands. When Ana is asked to do something she does not enjoy (e.g., writing or math), she runs to the corner and cries. The team puts strategies in place and although the plan seems like it would and should be successful, the number of times she shuts down doesn't seem to decrease.
>
> At a follow-up meeting, the teacher comments that things have improved. But when you look at the frequency data, you don't see an improvement. The teacher shares that although Ana is still shutting down, she is returning to her work much quicker than she had been. You revise the data collection to record how long the student's crying lasts. You discover that over two months, the student has moved from 45 minutes of crying to less than 5 minutes. This is amazing progress! She eventually stops this behavior altogether.

This example highlights the importance of knowing what type of data will be best for the context you are dealing with. Had you not considered duration, you might have changed the plans you had in place as you would not have recognized that they were showing success.

Collecting Frequency Data

Frequency data tracks how often something happens. It can be collected in many ways depending on what it is you are counting. Regardless of what data collection form you use, continue to aim for ease and simplicity of data collection.

If you want to know how often a behavior happens, look at frequency. If you want to know how long a behavior lasts, you need a way to track duration.

Start by looking at what is called ABC data:
- **A – Antecedent:** What occurs immediately before the behavior.
- **B – Behavior**
- **C – Consequences:** What happens immediately following the behavior.

We discussed consequences in Chapter 2 when considering the function of behavior, but it is important to remember that consequences do not specifically mean how a behavior is addressed by the teacher. Instead, consequences are anything that immediately follows a behavior (e.g., peers laughing, being removed from the room, the EA pulling away from the student, etc.).

Let's suppose you want to decrease a student's self-injurious behaviors. This example may be challenging as self-injury can sometimes be linked with sensory needs that may not show up as a pattern regardless of the data you are charting. Regardless, begin by looking at ABC data. In our example, the behavior would be when the student, Bora, punches himself (with a fisted hand) on his temple.

Begin by making sure the target behavior is understood by all involved.

Begin by making sure the target behavior is understood by all involved. Although Bora may also pick at his scabs and on a personal level some of the staff may see this as self-injurious behavior, for the purpose of the targeted behavior, you are looking specifically at times when he punches himself, with a closed fist, in the temple. With this specific behavior you would not need to write out "punched himself in the temple" as you are not recording other behaviors. But you would need to record the antecedent and the consequence. These could be written out, or you could create a checklist if you know the information you will regularly use.

If you were writing things out, it might look something like the chart in Figure 7.1. A sample BLM is provided in the appendix.

Student – *Bora* Direction – Record information each time you observe Bora punch himself (with a closed fist) in his temple.				
Date/Time	Antecedent	Behavior	Consequence	Initials

Figure 7.1 – Sample Data Collection Chart

The data/time column does not need to be very wide as this will only contain the date, 02/23 for example, and the time, such as 9:45. You also won't need to record anything in the behavior column as the behavior is explicitly defined and you are not recording multiple behaviors in this example. Instead, make the antecedent and consequence columns wider as you will be looking for more information about those aspects of the behavior.

If you know the types of antecedents or consequences you will be recording (either you know Bora well enough to predict these, you have started collecting data and have noted some patterns, or you are making an educated guess), this could be included in the chart in the form of a checklist, as in Figure 7.2 (on the next page). A sample BLM is provided in the appendix.

| Student – *Bora* |||||
| Direction – Record information each time you observe Bora punch himself (with a closed fist) in his temple. |||||
Date/Time	Antecedent	Behavior	Consequence	Initials
	☐ Presented with non-preferred task (_____) ☐ Asked to stop a preferred activity (_____) ☐ Coming in from outside ☐ Entering/leaving music/ gym ☐ Other: _____		☐ task/demand removed ☐ taken to sensory room ☐ sent home ☐ guidance/resource ☐ Other: _____	
Date/Time	Antecedent	Behavior	Consequence	Initials
	☐ Presented with non-preferred task (_____) ☐ Asked to stop a preferred activity (_____) ☐ Coming in from outside ☐ Entering/leaving music/ gym ☐ Other: _____		☐ task/demand removed ☐ taken to sensory room ☐ sent home ☐ guidance/resource ☐ Other: _____	

Figure 7.2 – Sample Data Collection Checklist

This form provides some options to check and/or circle. It also provides a few blanks so you can be more specific. If you select "Presented with a non-preferred task," specify what that is. A quick note in the blank will allow you to look for patterns in non-preferred tasks. With the option "Entering/leaving music/gym," the staff member can circle either entering or leaving, and they can also circle either music or gym. It is always important to leave "other" as an option as there may be things you didn't think of or were unaware of. It also allows for information such as "sub teacher" or "sub EA," which may be important factors.

> **TIP** You can create data collection forms as a team. As long as they accurately reflect the behavior and capture the information needed, there is no one official template to use. If you have found one that you really like but there are a few things missing, or it includes some things you don't need, create your own using that as your reference. (See the Recommended Resources section at the end of the book for more information.)

Once you gain an understanding of when and why Bora is engaging in the head-hitting behavior, you may be able to simplify the data collection process for a period of time while you evaluate the strategies you have put in place. For instance, suppose Bora never hits himself only one time. He punches himself quickly in the temple in a quick series of four or five punches. You may want to look specifically at a count to see if there is a reduction in this series of punches or an overall reduction in the number of times he hits himself each day.

You may be able to use a tally chart for this purpose, as shown in Figure 7.3. Sample BLMs with 15-minute and 30-minute increments, along with a blank sample tally chart, are provided in the appendix. The parameters will depend on the baseline data you have collected. If you know that Bora is punching himself multiple times within each half hour time block, you may want to look at creating a tally table in ten-minute blocks. If his head-hitting behavior is less frequent, you may be able to look at larger time blocks.

Student – *Bora* Direction – Record a tally mark for each time Bora punches himself (with a closed fist) in his temple.											
Date –											
9:00–9:10	9:10–9:20	9:20–9:30	9:30–9:40	9:40–9:50	9:50–10:00	10:00–10:10	10:10–10:20	10:20–10:30	10:30–10:40	10:40–10:50	

Figure 7.3 – Sample Tally Chart

In this example, the staff member can place a tally mark for each time Bora hits his head. This will provide a quick means of data collection. The times would be adjusted according to need.

Charting Frequency Data

It may be useful to chart the frequency data you collect to provide a visual of the behavior. This can be very rewarding for the team as it can sometimes better highlight successes than the raw data does. It can also help highlight patterns that may not have been identified from the raw data.

Suppose you have a primary aged student who is engaged in physically aggressive behavior toward peers: hitting, punching, and biting. The graph in Figure 7.4 represents data that has been collected over a block of time. A sample BLM of the chart below, along with a blank chart, are provided in the appendix.

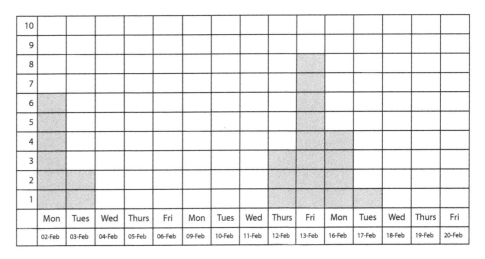

Figure 7.4 – Sample Chart of Frequency Data

Initially the data shown in Figure 7.4 looks very promising.

There is a noticeable reduction in behavior and six days during which there were no reported incidents of hitting, punching, or biting. A considerable relapse is noted following the period of non-incident. The raw data does not highlight any patterns in terms of what was occurring before the behavior, time of day, subject/task, day of the week, etc. An EA at the meeting in which the data is presented wonders if this is related to where the student was living during the week. The student alternates between their mother and father's home. Further data confirms the pattern that the student shows more aggressive behavior when living with one parent versus the other.

It is very important to ensure that patterns are not used to make assumptions or place judgments. The data does not allow you to determine that one home or parent is better than the other.

Suppose the student involved has a diagnosis of ASD and does not do well with lack of predictability. One home has a very unpredictable stepsibling. Once this is identified as a possible challenge for the student, both parents work together to try to create consistency between their home environments and the stepsibling is educated about the needs of her stepbrother. After some time and support both at home and at school, a permanent reduction in behavior is noted.

Using the Data

Once enough baseline data has been collected, the team will meet to look at the data and identify any patterns (e.g., is there a specific time of day, day of the week, subject area, etc. where behaviors occur the most often? Does the behavior appear to result in a specific consequence, such as attention or avoidance?). It is common to collect two weeks of baseline data before supports have been put in place to target the behavior.

Once any patterns are identified, preventative strategies can be put in place to help address any key areas that emerge from the data. Consequences can also be addressed, along with supporting any issues that may be exacerbating the situation. These could include educational strategies, medical supports, basic needs, and more.

> **TIP** Regardless of how you decide to track data, as long as everyone involved is on the same page and has a consistent understanding of the behavior and information being tracked, your data will serve as a solid guide in addressing challenging behavior.

Once the behavior is under control and the plans are occurring naturally, data collection may no longer be needed. If you find that things start to ramp up again, you can return to data collection for a period of time to regain your bearings.

Once any patterns are identified, preventative strategies can be put in place to help address any key areas that emerge from the data.

Student Data Collection

Having students collect their own data gives them an element of ownership and allows them to actively participate in their successes.

Depending on the student and the situation, it may be useful to have the student track their own data. This can add an element of ownership for the student and can also allow them to actively participate in their successes. There are many ways in which students can track their own behavior.

One example that is useful at the primary/elementary level involves students coloring in a chart. Try to use an image of something the student is interested in or something the student is working toward. For example, for Kasumi, a student who uses inappropriate language and demonstrates aggressive behavior, you could do the following:

> Use an image of a hockey stick or a thermometer, for example, and break it into sections to reflect the morning, the time between recess and lunch time, and the afternoon. Have Kasumi work with a staff member to identify the expectations for behavior. Green indicates no verbal or physical aggression. When creating a chart with Kasumi, use student-friendly language like "no bad words," and "no hitting or pushing." Yellow indicates that Kasumi starts to get upset but is successfully redirected by a staff member. In student-friendly language, use terms like "starting to get mad," "raising your voice," and "the teacher has to talk to you about your behavior." Red indicates that Kasumi cannot be redirected and becomes verbally or physically aggressive. This is expressed as times when "hitting" or "pushing" occurs or Kasumi uses "bad words."
>
> At the end of each time block, Kasumi reflects with a staff member to determine an appropriate color for that section of the hockey stick. She then colors in the section accordingly. For each time block that she is able to color green, she immediately receives five minutes of free time, which she most often use to play on a computer. This schedule of reinforcement works well for the staff members as well as the student.
>
> Kasumi can keep these sheets in her desk. By keeping these sheets and tracking them, you can look back to see a progression from predominantly red and yellow days to predominantly green and yellow days. You will eventually be able to move toward delayed reinforcement by offering her a larger reinforcer upon accumulating a set number of green days. You can also send the sheet home each day so Kasumi's parents/guardians can reinforce green days and she can share successes at home.

Here are some other strategies for students to collect their own data:

- Give the student a grid and stickers or a bingo dab for each appropriate behavior. Once they accumulate a pre-determined number of stickers/dabs, they access a pre-established reinforcement opportunity. For example, each time Sarah achieves five stickers, she and a friend can go to the reading corner and read one of their favorite books.
- Implement a plan where initially the student needs to obtain a set number of stickers (or whatever) to earn a desired activity. Once this is occurring regularly, raise the bar by upping their reinforcement each time they beat their previous score. For instance, if Roz earns the opportunity to listen to his favorite song each time he accumulates ten stickers, he can perhaps earn a set amount of time each time he accumulates more than ten stickers, or more than the number of stickers he received the day before. If he earns five stickers a period or ten stickers a time block, eventually look at a certain number of stickers a day and eventually even a week.

- If a student is highly reinforced by praise and recognition by adults, have them email or share their data with you every week to motivate them. For example, suppose you are working with Bella, a student who has ASD and is interested in computers. Make it a point to use computer time with Bella to reinforce her learning. Since she likes computers, she may enjoy emailing you a summary of her data at the end of each week. She is also likely to be motivated by getting to use the computer and receiving an email from you. You can praise Bella when her data for the week is good, and provide feedback for other times that aren't as good.

Success can be measured in many ways and data is an important part in measuring and illustrating success. When you are collecting data that is not shared directly with the student, try to keep this as simple as possible. When you are collecting data that you share with the student, or when you are supporting the student in collecting their own data, simple still works, but making it fun and appealing is also useful.

KEY IDEAS

- Although data is often the most useful tool in addressing challenging behavior, it is also the most underused.
- Make the data collection process as simple as possible.
- Consider the location of the data records, the timing of the data collection, and the accuracy of the data.
- Begin by collecting a week or two of baseline data, data you collect before putting strategies in place.
- Duration data and frequency data are two common types of data collected.
- When collecting frequency data, consider the antecedent, the behavior, and the consequences (ABC data).
- Use a data collection chart, checklist, or tally chart to track the behavior. (The appendix at the end of the book provides sample data collection BLMs. See also the Recommended Resources section for additional examples.)
- Charting frequency data provides a helpful visual of the behavior.
- After collecting baseline data, look at the data as a team to identify any patterns.
- It is sometimes useful to have the student track their own data.

8

Schedules, Routines, and Predictability

Predictability can be one of the most proactive strategies you can use. This is second nature to many teachers as we tend to be organizers, using agendas to record things like guest speakers, fire drills, assemblies, due dates, field trips, book buddies, and more. Teachers function best when they know what is going on, and your students are no different.

The difference between your students and you is in your ability to accommodate change. Most adults have the self-regulation skills necessary to change their plans and step out of routine without becoming emotionally charged. For some students this may not be the case. Many rely on the predictability and structure of their daily routine to give them a sense of control over their day. When this is disrupted, the result can be behavior issues.

Think about the level of push-back you might get following what may seem to be a simple issue, like an early dismissal. If your class did not get to go to gym yesterday because they were dismissed early, they may insist that they should have gym today as otherwise they will have music two days in a row. Sometimes even the smallest changes can have a large impact on students. And for the students who prefer gym to music, this can set them off and they may require support to get back on track.

> Many students rely on the predictability and structure of their daily routine to give them a sense of control over their day.

Visual Schedules

One of the best ways to promote predictability is to use a visual schedule. This tools outlines the daily schedule (e.g., classes, breaks, and specialist classes), while at the same time highlighting any changes or special activities. Many teachers incorporate a review of the day's events during their morning routine. Writing the date above your visual schedule as well as the day in the school cycle (if your school is on a day cycle, such as Day 1–6) can also be helpful.

Visual schedules typically consist of different pictures and/or words to represent the classes and activities of the day. Each picture is on its own card that is adhered in an easily accessible and visible area. The cards are usually attached in a temporary way so they can be easily repositioned. Velcro and sticky tac (the blue mounting putty, also called Tac N' Stick or Fun-Tak) are the most common methods used to attach the cards. Magnets also work, but note that they can scratch a white board. Some of your visuals may be specific to a particular student and may transition with them from grade to grade.

> **TIP** If you choose to use Velcro on your visual schedule, ensure that all staff members agree on which side of the Velcro is stuck to the board/wall and which is placed on the card. This will ensure that the cards can be easily transferred from class to class. An easy way to remember is using the expression "soft stays": The soft part of the Velcro (the looped part) stays on your wall or white board, and the harder or hooked part is placed on the cards.

Whole Class Visual Schedules

The most common place for a whole class visual schedule is at the front of the room on the white board.

When you think of visual schedules, you likely envision a whole class schedule. The most common place for a whole class visual schedule is at the front of the room on the white board. This makes it easy for students to see while at the same time it is readily available for you to access and reference throughout the day. Refer to the visual schedule frequently throughout the day when you start using it, such as at the beginning of the day and to introduce the transition between activities. Your frequent referencing will serve as a model for students.

For students who find it difficult to transition between activities, it may be useful to reference the upcoming change a few minutes prior to the transition. For example:

> You could say, "Okay boys and girls, when the big hand gets to the four we will set our paintings under the window and go to the book corner." Point to the painting and book corner cards on the visual schedule, then say something like, "Okay everyone, we are almost finished painting for today. Who can tell me what we will be doing when we finish painting?" Choose a volunteer, possibly even one of the students who struggles with transitions, to share what comes next or to come to the front of the room and demonstrate on the visual schedule what is coming next. This is a great time to reinforce the student for using the visual schedule if this is a goal for that student.

Individual Schedules

Although all students (and even the adults in your room) will benefit from a whole class schedule, some students may require a more hands-on experience with the schedule. It is not possible to always call on a particular student to come to the front of the room to model the transitions in your schedule, so if this is the level of support a student needs to be successful, try creating a personal or individual schedule for them. This may look very similar to the class schedule in terms of order and activities, but would be much smaller in size and would be immediately accessible to the student.

Select an individual visual schedule format that is easy to use.

Individual visual schedules take many different formats and need to meet your needs, the needs of your support staff (if there are any working with the student), and the needs of your student. There is no one best format. Ideally, select a format that you feel will be the easiest to use. If a visual schedule becomes too cumbersome it will not be used by anyone, which would be unfortunate for the student who requires this level of support to be successful throughout the day. Stay with the "keep it simple" philosophy.

Print

The first thing to consider is the student's level of functioning. If the student can read and write, try using a schedule that includes simple pictures (if needed) and print that provides a quick overview of the day. You may choose to have blanks on days where something special, or outside of the routine, is happening and work with the student to fill this in together. This would give you a bit of time to discuss the event, understand when it is happening in the day, and discuss anything you might want or need to experience success during that event. Filling in the blanks could also give the student the opportunity to copy the word (e.g., fire drill) or sound out the activity as they add it to their schedule. Or, you could have the student observe as the support person sounds it out and prints it in the schedule.

The most important goal is for the student to be able to successfully predict and understand their day.

The most important goal is for the student to be able to successfully predict and understand their day. If they can handle the academics of filling in a blank or two, that's great. But if this is an added stress that may hinder the success of the schedule, don't do it. There will be many other opportunities for the student to print or sound out words during the day. Remember, the visual schedule must work for all involved and needs to be as simple and easy as possible.

Visuals

If the student is not at a fluent or functional reading and writing level, use more detailed pictures and simple words on the cards.

If the student is not at a fluent or functional reading and writing level, use more detailed pictures and simple words on the cards. This will help ensure that the student can successfully understand and interact with their visual schedule. Having both pictures and words will also support them in beginning to understand print.

Most visuals are done using cartoon graphics. This may work for most students, but not all. Some students might not recognize that a stick figure represents an actual person, or that it is intended to represent them. If this is the case, a stick figure with a large circle in their hands would not represent gym for this student. And the stick figure with the large circle and the letters g-y-m beneath will likely not be successful either. If the student is at this level, you might want to take pictures of them engaged in each activity on their visual schedule.

To decide what visuals to include in the schedule, begin by reviewing your day. Create a list of all the things you might want on the student's schedule and think about how to represent them in pictures. Some will be easy, while others may be more difficult. For example, you could take a picture of the student in the gym for the gym card, perhaps holding a basketball. But before doing that, think about how flexible or inflexible the student is. If you have a picture of them in the gym with a basketball, are they going to expect to be playing with the basketball? Will they be okay if today they are hopping in hoola-hoops on the floor? Ultimately, you will need to make that call.

Create a list of all the things you might want on the student's schedule and think about how to represent them in pictures.

You may choose to take photos of the student in the gym doing activities or with equipment they will be using throughout the year. A resource teacher or support person could help with this if possible. Keep in mind that you don't want to have to sort through a huge number of photos to find the relevant one for a particular day, so use the minimum number of photos that works. Again, when and where possible, follow the "keep it simple" approach.

Another option is to include the student in only some of the photos, or perhaps a picture of the gym is enough. If the student recognizes the space as gym, you don't need to include the student in the picture. Similarly, if a photo of the play area for recess works for the student, it isn't necessary to include photos of the student on the slide or the swings. Choose what will work best for the student.

Make sure to choose appropriate images for the activities. For a fire drill, for example, you could use a photo of the fire bell on the wall for a fire drill, or a photo of the students lined up in their fire drill location. In this particular situation, a picture of the fire alarm might be best as it cannot be mistaken for something else. Your students lined up in their designated fire area may just look like a line up, such as for the end of the day. Try to avoid using visuals that will confuse, trigger, or upset the student.

If you are doing some initial teaching/discussions about an activity, take the time to incorporate the visual into your teaching. Suppose you are talking and teaching about fire drills:

Try to avoid using visuals that will confuse, trigger, or upset the student.

> Have a large visual for the front of the class. Hold it, point to it, and refer to it frequently and repeatedly while you talk/teach about fire drills as well as in the days preceding any drills that you are aware of. While this is occurring, the student should have their own individual fire drill visual. They can look at it when you are referencing the larger one for the class. You could also make this very explicit if needed. If so, you might say something like, "Donna, do you have a fire drill card?" or "Donna, show me/point to/hold up your fire drill card." Be sure to use the language "fire drill" when prompting the student. The more times they hear or reference it, the more they will develop their understanding.

You may also want to do a class fire drill practice. Point to your visual or hold it up while doing this. Have the student refer to theirs as well at the start and end of the fire drill practice, to link the whole process with the visual (i.e., hearing the alarm, lining up, leaving the class, going outside, returning to the classroom). Avoid taking the visual outside with you or having the student take it as you don't want this to become part of the process for them (e.g., you don't want the student to have to go back to the class to get their visual if the fire bell rings when the student is away from class or if a substitute teacher forgets to bring it with them).

Objects

If you have a student who does not yet recognize real-life pictures, you may need to create an object schedule for them. This will probably be a rare occurrence.

An object schedule outlines the day's events using objects to represent each activity.

An object schedule follows the same philosophy—a run down of the day's events—but it uses objects to represent each activity. This will be a little trickier than a visual schedule for several reasons:

- Objects are usually larger than pictures, so there may not be room to map out the whole day.
- Depending on the object, the student may wish to play with it instead of doing their work.
- It may be difficult to select one specific object to represent various activities (e.g., such as recess).

When selecting objects, there are the same risks as we discussed when taking a photo of the student with the basketball to represent gym time. Using a ball to represent gym time, for example, may give the student the idea that they are going to play ball, when in fact they will be playing with the parachute today. It would not be possible to put the parachute on the student's desk, and you want to keep your object consistent as this will help the student make the connection between the object and the activity. Instead, choose whatever object is most feasible and teach from there.

Make the connection between the objects and the activities very explicit for the student.

Make the connection between the objects and the activities very explicit for the student. This will require making frequent and repeated connections between the objects and the activities. For most students requiring this level of support, making the connection in the morning during review of the schedule and again when the activity is starting will not be enough. You may need to carve out time in the first few days and weeks where the student practices associating the objects with the activities. You can give the student the object, name it, and verbally make the association. You can also have the student take the object and match it to the activity or location.

If possible, it may be useful to display a second object by the location of the activity. For example, if you are using an empty stapler to represent the office, then have a stapler visually accessible in the office. When the student arrives at the office, hold the stapler up and match it with the officer stapler and say something like, "Yes, Donna, this is the office! Great job knowing that the stapler means we go to the office!" You will know best what language to use with the student, but keep it simple and to the point.

Reinforce the student when they successfully match the object to the activity or location.

Reinforce the student when they successfully match the object to the activity or location. Ensure that the students sees this as an activity (rather than thinking they are going to participate in the activity at that time) and experiences success as quickly as possible. Once the student understands what the objects represent (e.g., the ball means gym time, the spoon means lunch time, the paint brush means painting or crafts, etc.), you can begin to pair the object with a visual.

Given the student's level of functioning, you may wish to begin with real-life pictures. Continue using explicit teaching, but now have the student match the object to a picture of the activity, rather than having them map to the location or activity directly. Once the student masters this, you will be able to transition to a visual schedule, which is far more functional.

Progression for Schedules

Regardless of your starting point, eventually you want to transition to the least cumbersome schedule possible. Elementary teachers generally transition to a schedule represented by graphic (cartoon) visuals and print for both whole class and individual schedules, while in secondary school there is a move to word schedules where possible. Figure 8.1 shows the general progression for schedules.

Figure 8.1 – General Progression for Schedules

It is beneficial to begin each student at a level where they experience success.

Note that many students can start at the graphic image level. It is beneficial to begin each student at a level where they experience success. We would not recommend starting beneath their abilities as preceding levels are more cumbersome and would mean more transitions to get to a schedule at their functional level.

Creating Schedules

A number of factors should be considered when creating a schedule, including the type of images and text to use, how to organize the schedule, and where to keep it.

Choosing Images and Text

Given that you want to keep the schedule as simple as possible, here are a few things to keep in mind when choosing images and text at different stages of the progression.

Object:
- Does the object make sense for the activity it represents?
- Is the object familiar to the student?
- Is the object too generic or could it represent many things?
- Is the size of the object appropriate/manageable?

Real-life image:

- Does the photo accurately represent the activity?
- Do you want a photo of the location (e.g., music room) or of a specific activity/object (e.g., ukulele)?
- Does the student need to be in the photo?
- Does the student need to be in the room or with a specific object?

Graphic image:

- Does the visual accurately represent the activity?
- Do you want a general graphic (e.g., gym) or a specific one (e.g., gym items)?
- Do you want a graphic that is more functional or that is more appealing?

> **TIP** Be careful not to get caught up in the appearance of the graphic. You might tend to choose a graphic that stands out or that is bright or colorful because you like it best. However, this type of graphic may not be the most functional for the student. The student may require something that is simple and not visually overstimulating.

Figure 8.2 provides several examples of graphic images that could be chosen to represent gym time, as well as a rationale for each. It demonstrates the importance of weighing the pros and cons of each image when choosing them.

Graphic Image	Rationale
	Pros: • Simple • Not gender-specific • Easily identifiable as basketball Cons: • Figure is not "visually closed" and therefore may not be understood to represent a person • Specific to basketball versus gym
	Pros: • Simple • Non gender-specific • Could represent more than just basketball Cons: • Oddly-shaped person could be a distraction • Could be mistaken for recess or other play
	Pros: • Simple • Gender representation may be a benefit • Easily identifiable as basketball Cons: • Specific to basketball versus gym • Movement and shadow marks could be distracting

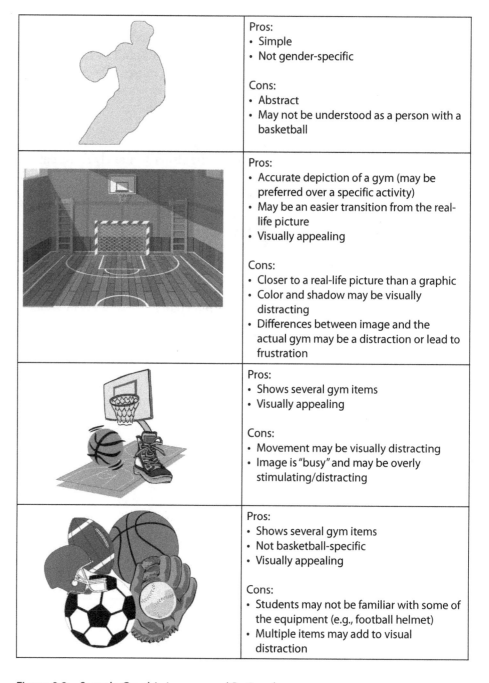

	Pros: • Simple • Not gender-specific Cons: • Abstract • May not be understood as a person with a basketball
	Pros: • Accurate depiction of a gym (may be preferred over a specific activity) • May be an easier transition from the real-life picture • Visually appealing Cons: • Closer to a real-life picture than a graphic • Color and shadow may be visually distracting • Differences between image and the actual gym may be a distraction or lead to frustration
	Pros: • Shows several gym items • Visually appealing Cons: • Movement may be visually distracting • Image is "busy" and may be overly stimulating/distracting
	Pros: • Shows several gym items • Not basketball-specific • Visually appealing Cons: • Students may not be familiar with some of the equipment (e.g., football helmet) • Multiple items may add to visual distraction

Figure 8.2 – Sample Graphic Images and Rationales

As you can see, there are many things to consider when selecting visuals to support students. Although we are typically drawn to interesting and colorful graphics, keep in mind that the things that often make a visual appealing may also be distracting or confusing for students.

Print:

- Is the font size adequate so it is visually accessible to the student?
- Is the font type clear?
- Is the font readable for the student? Not all students may be able to read cursive, so a script font may not be appropriate.
- Should you capitalize the first letter?

- Should you use all-caps or should you model text the student would encounter in reading materials?
- Does bold, underline, or italics help the readability of the text?
- Do you want any of the text in color?

It is easy to get caught up in the fun and flare of images and texts. We like things to be visually appealing, but this is sometimes at the cost of their functionality. When in doubt, focus on function. And, as always, the "keep it simple" philosophy can help you decide when pictures and text fonts are most functional.

Chunking Schedules

A whole class schedule typically represents the entire day. You can review it briefly at the start of the day, highlight anything out of the norm, and proceed with your day as usual. For students who benefit from individual schedules, the whole day may be too overwhelming or too cumbersome. And as mentioned earlier, a whole day schedule would not be possible with objects. Given this, you may need to break a schedule into chunks.

Presenting one activity at a time is not beneficial as it eliminates the ability of the student to see and understand (predict) what is coming next. At the very least, include two activities. If this is the route you choose, recognize that it means a lot of work for you, the student, or a support person as you will need to continuously add the next event to the schedule.

There may be some natural breaks in your day that would work well as breaks in the schedule. Try breaking the day into three chunks: a morning section (from the start of the day until morning recess), a mid-day section (from the end of morning recess until lunch), and an afternoon section (from the end of lunch to the end of the day).

This type of schedule chunking is useful for several reasons:
- It aligns with natural breaks in the day.
- The sections are not so large as to be overwhelming.
- If the student has a rough part in their day, it can feel like a clean slate when moving to a new section of the day.
- The end points in the schedule (i.e., recess, lunch, end of day) align well with possible reinforcement opportunities.

Another consideration when thinking about chunking a daily schedule is staff changes. If the student is receiving support from more than one person, it may work nicely to have each support person review the section of the day they will be there for. For example, if you have two EAs supporting a student, you could split the schedule for when they change up. In this way, the morning EA reviews their time with the student, and the second EA begins their time with the student by reviewing the rest of the day's events. This is not the same as a natural break in the day, but is a legitimate break in the student's day so it still makes sense. It also allows for the same "fresh slate" we discussed earlier if the student had any issues or conflicts earlier in the day.

Choosing the Schedule Location

We previously discussed the need for an individual visual schedule to be physically accessible. Where to best place it depends on many things, including how

Try breaking a schedule into three chunks: morning, mid-day, and afternoon.

Consider staff changes when thinking about chunking a daily schedule.

many work areas the student has, the size of the visual schedule, the size of the student's desktop, available wall space, and the need to transport the schedule.

You may be picturing the visual schedule as a neat vertical arrangement of cards running along the side of the student's work surface, or a horizontal row across the top of the workspace. Although this location is accessible, it also presents several challenges:

- Items on the student's workspace may cover the schedule, and it may be frustrating to move these items each time the student references the schedule.
- The visuals may move or become detached.
- Custodians may not wish to have anything adhered to the desk as it would make cleaning the desk more difficult.
- Food and dirt may get lodged in and around the schedule, and spills may damage it.
- End-of-year clean up may be an issue.
- Taping the schedule down eliminates the ability to move or change the schedule when aspects of the day change.
- It would be difficult to take the schedule to other work areas or classes.

Make sure the schedule is visually accessible as well as physically accessible.

As ideal as the desktop may seem, you may have to look at other options. Wall space is something to consider, particularly if there is a space that allows for easy access for the student and that is not being used to display other things. Make sure the schedule is visually accessible as well as physically accessible. If there are a lot of things on the wall in that area, it may be too visually distracting for the student. Wall space can be a viable option, but several of the challenges listed above are still present, particularly around taking the schedule to other work areas or classes.

Another option is using a binder to display a student's visual schedule. Represent the student's day in two columns on the front of the binder, one column for the morning portion of the day and the second for the afternoon. Inside the binder, provide page dividers with several strips of soft Velcro running vertically down the page. The page dividers are optimal because of their thickness (rather than using paper). If you are frequently pulling visuals off and onto the Velcro, you will need something sturdy to withstand a high level of handling.

Try using a binder to display a student's visual schedule.

Use several dividers in the binder to hold visuals, ranging from the most common classes and activities to special activities and events. For example:

- The first divider holds regular morning activities.
- The second contains visuals for regular afternoon activities.
- The third offers visuals for special events and activities.
- The fourth has visuals for preferred activities or reinforcers.

Each morning, have the student and an EA (if available) select visuals to represent the day. The student chooses the visual from the appropriate divider in the binder and places it on the front. During this time, the student and the EA can discuss anything that may be happening outside of the regular routine. As the student progresses through the day, they remove each visual upon completion and put it back in the binder. This gives the student a sense of ownership over the day.

There are many advantages to using a binder to display a visual schedule:

- It is completely portable so it can travel with the student from class to class or work area to work area.

- It remains with the student for special classes and can even be taken to special activities and events.
- It can be kept in the student's desk (if needed) and pulled out frequently for review.
- It contains and organizes all the visuals needed so there is no challenge with storing or finding visuals when needed.

Make modifications to the binder to meet your student's needs.

Although a binder may work well for some students, it may not be the solution for others. You may need to make some tweaks to make it more effective. For instance:

- Use one column if two columns are too much for the student.
- Leave the cover of the binder free and have each section of the schedule on its own divider.
- Use a larger binder or folder if the student uses real pictures instead of graphic visuals (which are usually small).

Including a divider for preferred activities may be effective for some students. For instance, a student may have two preferred activities scheduled into the day, one at the end of each schedule block (i.e., one before lunch and one before the end of the day). These activities are not "earned" but are built right into the schedule. It can be motivating for some students to choose preferred activities each morning and then see them coming up on the schedule. It also gives the teacher and EA some leverage as they can prompt the student verbally and visually about the upcoming activity. They can point to the visual of the preferred activity and say something like, "Let's keep going, we only have two more things to do before we get to play with the slime."

> **TIP** Make sure to use a format works for you, your student, and your context, aiming for as simple and as non-cumbersome as possible.

Substitute Teachers and Support Staff

For many students with behavioral challenges, having a substitute teacher can be challenging. In terms of predictability, a substitute teacher is not part of the regular routine. This in and of itself can cause challenges.

Make sure to share the student's schedule with the substitute teacher.

> **TIP** Ensure that the student's schedule is communicated to the substitute teacher. This is how the student's day begins and facilitating this process as regularly as possible will help the student feel like the day will follow the regular routine.

If you know in advance that there is going to be a substitute teacher in your classroom, either for you or for an EA, it may be beneficial to share this with the class or the student prior to it happening. You may wish to use a visual to represent a substitute teacher, which could be put at the top of the whole class visual schedule at the end of the day. This provides an opportunity to remind students about the next day's change in staff and serves as a visual reminder when they return in the morning. This level of predictability is essential for some students. For other students, knowing this in advance can ramp up their anxiety. You know your students best, so make your decisions based on their needs.

Ensuring the Success of Visual Schedules

Explicitly teach the visual schedule and refer to it frequently throughout the day.

One of the biggest stumbling blocks with visual schedules is lack of use. In some situations, an incredible amount of time and energy is put into mapping out the schedule and creating the visuals, but it is not frequently referenced or used throughout the day. Referencing a visual schedule in frustration when a student is having difficulty transitioning from a specific activity will not teach the student to predict and work though transitions.

> **TIP** You need to explicitly teach the visual schedule and refer to it frequently throughout the day, regardless of the student's success at navigating the schedule on any given day.

Another issue involves prematurely assuming that the student no longer needs the visual schedule. When a student becomes good at transitioning through the day and doesn't appear to reference the schedule much, you may sometimes assume this means the student no longer needs the schedule. Instead, it is more likely that the student has mastered the schedule, which is different.

Consider the following non-student example:

> Sam is always late getting to work, shows up late for meetings, and is generally late for anything with a time expectation. He gets a watch and sets a few timers for specific daily time requirements. After a couple of weeks, he is getting to all his commitments on time and being late is no longer an issue. In this context Sam has mastered the use of his watch to support his needs. However, we do not assume that Sam no longer needs his watch. If we take away his watch, he will very likely revert to being late. The same philosophy applies for visual schedules.

When students have mastered their schedule and no longer require the same amount of hands-on work with it, transition to a less invasive schedule but do not abandon the schedule all together. You may be able to move to a visual schedule that is fixed to a nearby wall rather than one that is transported to all classes, referencing it if and as needed. Or, perhaps the student can transition from an individual schedule to the whole class schedule. Either of these options allows the student to access a schedule if and when needed. If you remove the schedule completely, the student will not have access to this support.

KEY IDEAS

- Schedules, routines, and predictability are proactive strategies to help give students a sense of control over their day.
- Visual schedules consist of different pictures and/or words to represent the classes and activities of the day.

- Make whole class visual schedules visible and accessible so you can refer to them often throughout the day.
- Individual schedules can take many different formats, including print, visuals, and objects.
- Eventually you want to transition to the least cumbersome schedule possible (e.g., object to real-life image to graphic image to print).
- When creating a schedule, consider the types of images and text you will use, breaking the schedule into chunks, and where you will keep the schedule to ensure easy access.
- Ensure that the student's schedule is communicated to substitute teachers and support staff.
- Explicitly teach the visual schedule and refer to it frequently throughout the day.

9

Visual Supports

By using visual supports, you are creating a visual prompt to support and guide student behavior.

In addition to visual schedules, there are many other ways to use visuals to support behavior management. Some of the more common ones include social stories, scripts, first/then boards, and choice boards. By using visual supports, you are creating a visual prompt to support and guide student behavior.

As teachers, we often prompt or redirect students verbally. Although this may be effective for some students, verbal cues are only present for as long as you are saying the words. Your hope is that your verbal cue remains in the mind of the student, but there are no guarantees that this will happen. In addition, if the student is actively attempting to keep your verbal cue in mind, this can take away from the attention you want them to invest in the task at hand.

In contrast, a visual cue remains after it is referenced. In the same way you use anchor charts and instructional displays to prompt students about concepts, expectations, and more, you can use visuals to support students (whole class or individually) with behavior. Visual materials allow for easy reference by staff, but also provide support to students throughout the day with and without your referencing them. (See the Recommended Resources section at the end of the book for more information about visuals.)

Social Stories

A social story is a short, student-friendly story that is created to support a student in understanding the perspective of others.

Social stories may seem like an odd choice to start as they are more complex than a picture or cue on the wall. Regardless, social stories (first created by Carol Gray) are very important for developing perspective and understanding of contexts. A social story is a short, student-friendly story that is created to support a student in understanding the perspective of others. Although you could have social stories for many situations, it is best to use only one story at a time otherwise you run the risk of the social story losing its effectiveness.

Social stories are generally read to the student whose behavior you are targeting. However, if a social story is applicable to the whole class, you can read it to everyone. Make sure to include some one-on-one readings with the student until they "know it by heart" and can read/recite the important parts independently. This will help them create an internal dialogue related to the expected behavior and/or strategies outlined in the story. The student's age and cognitive ability will matter, but that is why you should specifically choose the language and pictures for the student the story is intended for.

Let's use an example to understand when, how, and why you would use a social story.

> Many students have issues on the playground. Turn taking, physical contact, lack of structure, and never-ending changes to game play can all be sources of stress for some students. Mitchum, in Grade 2, has been having trouble keeping his hands to himself. He is frequently directed to sit on the bench or is taken into the school for hitting and pushing his peers. Mitchum has a behavior plan and receives reinforcement at the end of each outside break if there have not been any issues involving hitting or pushing. You also want to create a social story for him so he will understand how his behaviors make his peers feel. It will include strategies and suggestions for Mitchum as alternate options to hitting and pushing.

Creating a Social Story

The basic structure for a social story is as follows:
- Introduce the issue.
- Explain how it makes others feel.
- Provide alternatives.
- End with how the alternatives will make people feel.

Make sure the social story ends positively as this is likely what will stay in the student's memory the longest.

Make sure the social story ends positively as this is likely what will stay in the student's memory the longest. For instance, the student will have a greater chance of having a successful recess if they are focused on "When I keep my hands to myself my friends will be happy" rather than "If I hit or push I will go to the office." Although both statements may be true, one statement focuses on the preferred outcome (in our example, Mitchum keeping his hands to himself), while the other focuses on the negative behaviors.

Be sure to use student-friendly language and to be clear and concise. You don't want your message to be lost in excessive, unnecessary language. Be purposeful with your visuals as well. Although this is not always a common practice, try targeting a visual from the story and displaying a copy of it in the classroom. You may even choose to target a specific page from the story and display both the visual and print material in the classroom. Be strategic in where you display the story. You want it easily referenced but also visible in the area where is it most needed, the recess transition area in our example. One option is to post it beside the classroom door where staff can refer to it as students line up to go outside. Consider posting it lower than other visuals in the class so it is eye level for the students. You want Mitchum to see it as he leaves the classroom for each break.

Print the story in color and use sturdy cardstock. You can also laminate the story and then use a binder ring to hold it together. Make three copies of the story: one for the classroom, one for the EA (if applicable), and one for home. Having parents/guardians as partners in behavior change is key, as we have discussed previously. It can be beneficial for the family to look at the story with the student and discuss what it means, talk about the alternate suggestions, and debrief at the end of the day.

You may also wish to consult with support people for feedback, including the resource teacher and the EA, as they may have some insights into alternative behavior suggestions, pictures and language that would appeal to the student, and more. You may also have a resource teacher or behavior resource teacher at your school who can create the story for you.

> **TIP** Many social stories are available online and you may find one that suits your needs. However, creating your own social stories allows you to tailor all information specifically to the student and the issues you are addressing. This also allows you to select specific visuals to support the story.

Introducing the Story

Read the story many times throughout the first few days and weeks when you first introduce it.

Read the story many times throughout the first few days and weeks when you first introduce it. In addition, read it prior to each break. For example:

Read the story to Mitchum until he can read it independently or recite it with you. When he can read or recite it, you will know he has internalized it, or at least the words. If you have used language at his level and paired it with specific pictures, there is a greater chance that Mitchum also knows the meaning and message of the story.

Even when the student knows the story, both the words and meaning, the student may still struggle with the target behavior. This is understandable as there is likely more at play than just a lack of understanding. There could be issues of impulsivity, limited emotional regulation, lack of replacement behaviors, or more. This is why you should include alternate behaviors in the social story and also have a reinforcement system in place.

Including Peers

In addition to the supports in place directly for the student, you may also want to look at peer understanding and support. For example:

> Discuss with the class how recess can be challenging for some students and look at ways they can support each other on the playground. Provide strategies, both actions and statements, that students could use to support Mitchum when interacting with him. Given that Mitchum has been aggressive with his peers, providing the other students with supports and strategies may also help reduce any anxiety or tension between him and his peers.

Depending on the social story you are using, it may be beneficial to read it aloud to the whole class. Continue reading the story individually with the student as well, but a whole class approach may help normalize the problem behavior, and this may help the student feel as though they are not being targeted. This will all depend on the context of the class and the individual students.

Depending on the social story you are using, it may be beneficial to read it aloud to the whole class.

> **TIP** Incorporating all the students in the class, when possible, also lends itself to class discussions that help build perspective, as well as class debriefing on days where things don't go well. In addition, the story and the posted visual from the story may be helpful to other students, even those you didn't realize were struggling.

Sample Story

Let's look at possible story for Mitchum. Remember that he is in Grade 2 and his reading is slightly below grade level. You want to keep the following criteria in mind when writing the story:

- Make sure to write clearly and concisely.
- Outline the issue that needs to be addressed.
- Consider the peer perspective.
- Offer suggestions for alternate behavior options.
- End the story with a positive perspective.

You can write the whole story on one page, which is not uncommon, or you can include a picture and a few lines of text on multiple pages.

Given Mitchum's grade level and the idea that you want to read the story aloud with the whole class from time to time, and considering that you want to use a key page from the story as a visual, we are going to use a storybook approach with a half-page format for Mitchum's story. Figure 9.1 (on the next page) provides an example of what the story for Mitchum may look like.

Playing Outside at Recess and Lunch 	At school, we go outside at recess and lunch. I like going outside. I have fun playing with my friends.	 Sometimes I get mad when I am playing with my friends. When I get mad I might hit or push my friends.
 My friends do not like it when I hit or push them. My friends feel sad when I hit and push them.	I will try not to hit or push my friends when I get mad. The next time I get mad, I can: ☺ Ask a friend for help ☺ Count to ten ☺ Walk away ☺ Take a break ☺ Play something different ☺ Talk to the duty teacher	 Everyone will be happy when there is no hitting and no pushing. We will have fun playing when everyone is happy.

Figure 9.1 – Sample Social Story

Note that the last page of this story focuses on positive peer interactions. You may wish to choose to display this page from the story in the classroom. Put a simple border around the page and centre the text to help make it look like a poster, as shown in Figure 9.2.

Everyone will be happy when there is no hitting and no pushing. We will have fun playing when everyone is happy.

Figure 9.2 – Sample Story Page to Display in the Classroom

Checklist for Creating an Effective Social Story

Ensure the social story meets all the requirements outlined in this section:
- ☐ Ensure it is clear and concise.
- ☐ Use student-friendly language.
- ☐ Introduce the issue.
- ☐ Explain how the behavior makes others feel.
- ☐ Provide alternative behaviors.
- ☐ Explain how alternative behaviors will make people feel.
- ☐ End on a positive note.

In addition, here are some other tips for using social stories:
- Make sure the student interacts frequently with the story.
- Read the story to the student often in the first few days and weeks, particularly before the usual time the problem behavior occurs.
- Use the story to support discussions and follow up or when debriefing with the student.
- Remember that social stories are only a small part of any behavior plan.

See the Recommended Resources at the end of the book for more information about social stories.

Scripts

Scripts are similar to social stories, except that they do not include peer perspectives. Scripts are not about understanding how others feel or how they may respond to certain behaviors or contexts. Instead, they outline a process for a particular student. Scripts can be used in many contexts, including regular routines and play.

Visual Routines for Specific Times of the Day

Visual scripts can help students complete specific daily routines.

For many students, completing specific daily routines can be challenging. And when those routines are at the beginning of the day, this can sometimes start the day off on the wrong foot. Consider the following example:

Toni is a Grade 1 student who has problems putting her things away when she first arrives in class. She often gets distracted and takes longer than the rest of her peers to put her things away. This is frustrating for the staff, and constantly being redirected is frustrating for Toni. By the time she is ready for her day, she is already emotionally dysregulated.

Create a visual script for Toni consisting of a vertical strip of photos, each indicating what comes next in her morning routine. For instance, her visual routine might consist of the following photos:
- Her coat on a hook and the text "hang up coat"
- Her lunch box on the shelf with the text "put lunch box away"
- Her backpack on a hook with the text "put backpack away"
- Her sneakers on her feet with the text "put sneakers on"
- A star with the text "great job!"

Because of Toni's age and cognitive ability, use photos of her actual items. This will be easier for Toni to identify than generic pictures or graphics. Laminate the script and place it on the wall beside Toni's coat hook. Include a dry erase marker beside it so that Toni can cross off each step as it is completed. Although this is not necessary, it can be motivating. The last picture, the star and "great job!" statement, indicates that Toni can chose a reinforcer for completing her routine. Offer her a choice from three very quick reinforcers.

In this example, the visuals provide Toni with prompts to complete her routine without the staff having to continuously redirect her verbally (which Toni had felt was "nagging" or "growling"). If Toni requires redirecting, staff can verbally redirect her to the visual, or physically redirect her by gesturing or pointing to the visual. By redirecting Toni to the visual routine, she will become less dependent on staff telling her what to do and more independent. This will help reduce everyone's frustration. Also, by providing reinforcement upon completion of her routine, Toni will become more motivated to move quickly through the routine. Not only does this speed things up, it also provides a positive and successful start to the day.

Visual scripts can be helpful for other key times of the day as well, including coming in/going out for recess/lunch, transitioning to specialist classes, and end-of-day routines. Visual scripts can also help with work and task completion. In addition, visual scripts are very useful with various hygiene routines, including toileting behaviors, brushing teeth, taking a bath, getting ready for bed, and more.

> **TIP** Visual scripts can be very complex. If too many visuals are included, they can be overwhelming. Remember that less is more. Keep things as simple as possible.

Visual Routines for Play Time

Visual scripts can have a place in play. Outside play is often challenging for students with behavioral difficulties. As mentioned earlier, issues include turn taking, physical contact, lack of structure, and never-ending changes to game play, to name a few. Some students also don't like going outside because of issues of temperature (e.g., too hot, too cold, too windy, wet grass, etc.), some don't know how to access the equipment (e.g., not sure what to do on different parts of the play equipment, can't pump their own swing, etc.), and some simply prefer indoor activities.

Try using a visual script to support the student with outside play and motivate them to engage with various outdoor activities.

Regardless of the reason, a student who is upset about having to go outside is already in a state of emotional dysregulation before even getting outside. This is not optimal heading into a non-preferred task or activity. Try using a visual script to support the student with outside play and motivate them to engage with various outdoor activities. Start by creating visuals of outside activities (take photos if needed or use visuals/graphics depending on the needs of your student) and then discuss these with the student. You may wish to go outside when it is not recess/lunch to physically map the activity with the photo. For example, if the photo shows a student on a swing, show the student the picture and then push them on the swing.

Once you are sure the student understands the pictures, have them choose three activities prior to going outside. These could be on a binder ring or whatever is easiest for the support staff or duty teacher to carry. The student flips the card each time they complete the activity. Include a fourth card that indicates success, such as a star, a smiley face, or a thumbs up. Initially allow the student to go indoors once they have completed the activities. This will quickly build success. Eventually you will put a quantity or time on the activities.

Consider the following example:

> If the student chooses the slide, have them go down the slide four times instead of just once. Increase your expectations very slowly. Eventually your goal will be to have the student stay outside for the full duration of the break and receive the reinforcement when they get indoors. This will be accomplished by increasing the time they interact with each activity and/or adding activities to the routine.

Similar visuals can be used to support many play-based activities. For students who struggle with peer interactions, visuals to support play can help promote positive peer interactions and relationships.

Visuals to Support Behavioral Expectations

Visuals can also be used to support a student in understanding and meeting behavioral expectations. This type of visual is very common and we see examples everywhere—no smoking signs, no pets, no shirts no service, no food or drinks. In terms of school, think about times, activities, and locations where specific behavior is expected. For instance, in the library we may post "quiet voices" signs, in the hallway we may have "no running" signs, and we may have signs in the classroom that support behavior (e.g., many teachers use the visual of a stoplight with behavior examples listed beside the green, amber, and red light).

The bus is another area where visual cues/supports may be beneficial to support student behavior. The bus can be a very challenging environment for students for a multitude of reasons:

- The bus can be loud and chaotic.
- The ride may be long and the student may become bored over time.
- Other students/behaviors might trigger the student.
- The student may be on medication that wears off by the time they are on the bus.
- The bus is unstructured.
- The student may or may not like/know the student sitting with them.

Although the bus is outside of your responsibilities, when the bus ride doesn't go well, there is a high probability that your day will not go well. As a result, it is well worth your time to support the student on the bus if possible.

A visual of the bus expectations may be helpful. Visuals representing "I sit in my seat," "I use an indoor voice," and "I keep my hands to myself" taped to the wall or window where the student sits provide a visual prompt for the student and give the bus driver something to reference. You could also create tokens that the bus driver can give the student at the end of each successful bus ride. Parents can provide reinforcement for tokens received on the afternoon bus rides, and you can provide reinforcement each morning the student comes in with a token. Depending on the student, you can also consider offering reinforcement for a certain number of tokens.

First/Then Boards

First/then boards are very simple visuals that direct a student to complete a task or activity and illustrate what reinforcement they will receive upon completion of that task or activity. A first/then board usually has two squares, side by side, as shown in Figure 9.3. The first square has a piece of Velcro in the centre and the word "First" either at the top or the bottom. The second square has a piece of Velcro in the centre and the word "Then" either at the top or the bottom (wherever "First" is located). The student then attaches images to the board to represent what they need to do before they get a reinforcer.

First	Then

Figure 9.3 – Sample First/Then Board

First/then boards work well if the student and staff member fill them in together.

First/then boards work well if the student and staff member fill them in together. And it can be beneficial to start with the "then" section of the card as this highlights the positive for the student. When the student determines what they would like for a reinforcer (try asking "What are you working for?"), have them put the visual on the "then" section of the card. Reference the reinforcer when putting the "first" visual on the card. For example:

Gretta selects a puzzle as her reinforcer. You can say something like, "Okay Gretta. We will build your puzzle as soon as we read our book." While you are saying this, place the visual of the book in the "first" section.

If the student knows that the "first" activity will be based on a routine or visual schedule, you don't need to begin with the "then" section of the board. For instance:

If the student knows what is coming, allow them to put it on the first/then card if they would like. Then focus on the reinforcer by saying something like, "Yes Gretta, we will be reading our book next. What would you like to do when we finish reading our book?"

First/then boards are often used for non-preferred tasks, so try to focus on the "then" aspect.

Keep in mind that first/then boards are often used for non-preferred tasks, which is why you should try to focus on the "then" aspect. For example:

> You may need to prompt Gretta to keep working if she becomes distracted or disinterested in the book. The first/then board provides a visual reminder for Gretta about the reinforcement that is coming. You can also reference this by pointing or gesturing to the first/then board. Use language like, "When we finish our book we can build our puzzle," or "Only two pages left and then we get to build our puzzle!" Remember, because Gretta picked the "then" activity, it is likely to be reinforcing for her.

Choice Boards

We have referred to student choice several times in this book in terms of selecting their reinforcers, as well as selecting activities. Offering students choices, when possible, gives them a sense of control over the activities in their day. This can be very helpful in navigating challenging situations. Consider the following non-school example:

> I recently took my daughter to the dentist to fix a cracked tooth. She was very much hoping it could be fixed using the laser as she knew this would mean she didn't need a needle. Upon inspection, the dentist determined that the laser was not an option. My daughter was very upset about getting a needle. We offered her the choice of the laughing gas, the pink numbing cream, or the blue numbing cream. She asked about the creams and ended up using both. Although this didn't change the fact that she was fearful and upset about the needle, it did give her some level of comfort. Choice doesn't eliminate the things we don't like, it just sometimes makes them more tolerable.

Choice boards offer students choice, and therefore control, over some elements of their day.

Choice boards offer students choice, and therefore control, over some elements of their day. Recall the example of the visual routine for outside play that suggested the student choose three activities. For this student, you may have a board that includes all the possible outside activities, and they select three from this. However, a full board of options may be visually too much for the student to take in, the choices may cause the student anxiety, or it may just take too much time for the student to choose between so many options. Whatever the reason, try narrowing down the options. Some suggestions include:

- Select several more-likely options and offer the student a reduced choice board.
- Organize visuals into categories (e.g., equipment, games, peer play) and have the student select one from each category.
- Limit the number of options available in each category.
- Display all three categories at once or display the categories one at a time to keep choice-making focused.

These decisions will depend on what works best for you and your student.

Suppose a student is struggling in gym class. Use a choice board to support them by creating visuals for three categories: warm-up exercises, activities, and cool-down exercises. Initially the student chooses one activity from each category, with one minute assigned to warm-up and cool-down exercises, and five minutes assigned to the activities. Gradually increase the warm-up and cool-down exercises to three exercises each for a total of five minutes, and increase the activities to 15 minutes. Depending on the focus of the lesson, the student may focus on the same activity for the 15 minute duration, or may select several activities related to the unit.

For example, suppose the class is working on basketball. The activity choices for the student might include dribbling, throwing and catching, and shooting hoops. These activities could be done individually, with a partner, or in a small group. Depending on the student and the context, you may decide which activities are individual, partner, or small group. You can categorize the choice board in this way and the student selects the activities knowing which are individual, which are with a partner, and which involve a small group. You may also allow the student to determine if they want to work alone or with others.

We cannot overstate the importance of choice. When students feel like they have control throughout their day, they feel a sense of ownership over their day. This will, in turn, help them buy into the supports in place. Choice boards for activities (as described above) and for reinforcers are great ways to incorporate choice into a student's day. And keep in mind that students are not getting to choose NOT to do something, they are just choosing some of the aspects involved (e.g., they are not choosing whether or not to do silent reading; they are choosing whether to sit and read in class or to read elsewhere). Sometimes choice gives the students the illusion of control, and that's not a bad thing.

KEY IDEAS

- Social stories, scripts, first/then boards, and choice boards are helpful visuals to support behavior management.
- A social story is a short, clear, and concise story that uses student-friendly language to support a student in understanding the perspective of others. (See the Recommended Resources section for more information about social stories.)
- Social stories do not generally change behavior in and of themselves, but are used in combination with other strategies to support student behavior.
- The structure for a social story is: introduce the issue; explain how it makes others feel; provide alternatives; and end with how the alternatives will make people feel.
- Print the story in color and use sturdy cardstock or laminate it.
- Creating your own social stories allows you to tailor all information specifically to the student and the issues you are addressing.
- Scripts are similar to social stories, except that they do not include peer perspectives.
- Scripts outline a process for a particular student, such as routines for specific times of the day.
- Visuals provide the student with prompts to complete a routine without staff having to continuously redirect them verbally. (See the Recommended Resources section for more information about visuals.)
- Visuals can also be used to support a student in understanding and meeting behavioral expectations.
- First/then boards are very simple visuals that direct a student to complete a task or activity and illustrate what reinforcement they will receive upon completion.
- Choice boards offer students choice, and therefore control, over some elements of their day.

When students feel like they have control throughout their day, they feel a sense of ownership over their day.

10

Timers

You can use timers for setting expectations, to motivate, and to reinforce positive behaviors.

Timers can be an excellent tool to support behavior management. At the very basic level, you can use timers to set expectations. You can also use timers to motivate and reinforce positive behaviors. You can use them discretely with students on an individual basis or as a tool for the whole class. Which options are best will depend on you, your students, and your context.

Types of Timers

Before we examine *how* to use timers to support behavior management, we want to stress the need for timers to be visual. Announcing the passage of time, or any other verbal reference to time, is likely to be counterintuitive. Many students have been on the receiving end of "in a minute" or "just a second," which could well be followed by half an hour or more of wait time. This results in many students having a very inaccurate understanding of time, particularly when they are younger. Visual timers solve this problem as the passage of time and/or the amount of time remaining is visually displayed.

Many forms of visual timers may be useful depending on your context, ranging from sand timers, to wind up timers, to digital timers, and with many options in between. Sand timers alone have come a long way over the years. You can get sand timers in various time increments, as well as with different colors of sand. You can also get sand timers that contain grains of metal instead of sand. These sit on a magnetic block and the grains of metal create interesting formations when they land in the bottom of the timer.

Another type of timer is made with oils that slowly bubble their way to the top/bottom. These would be similar to a lava lamp in their appeal and come in many colors. Just keep in mind that some of the more fascinating timers can be more of a distraction than a tool of focus. As fascinating as the lava lamp type of timer is, this may be something you let students use to keep track of their free time or reinforcement time rather than for timing their assigned tasks/activities.

Wind-up timers come in many shapes and sizes. These range from dollar store timers shaped like various vegetables, to larger clock-sized magnetic timers that are generally used with the entire class. Some wind-up timers contain a colored window that displays the time remaining and that shrinks with the passage of time. These timers are very effective for displaying how much time is left for a given task/activity. They are also available in battery operated (versus wind up) versions and can be purchased in both individual and whole-class size.

Digital timers range from simple dollar store timers to more complex versions. And again, these can be purchased in an individual size or in a size large enough to be used with the entire class. One benefit to the small, individual sized timers from the dollar store is that they are affordable enough to have many of them in your class. You might give them to select students who need this support or to groups during group work, or you may choose to set one for you and one for a student when giving them a set amount of time for something. Consider the following example:

> Jack often asks to go to the restroom but then wanders randomly around the school, often being gone for almost 20 minutes. Begin by discussing the importance of communicating his needs. If he needs to use the restroom, you expect him back in three minutes; if he needs a break, you will both determine the amount of time needed at the time of the request. Jack and you both set your timers before he leaves (whether for the restroom or for a break). You setting a timer lets Jack know that you will be keeping track of his time. This serves two purposes: It eliminates the possibility of him adding minutes to his timer, and it also cues you if he is gone longer than expected. If this is the case, you needs to have someone check on him to make sure he is okay and to prompt him to return.

Online timers are also very popular. Many teachers project these onto their white boards and use them for the whole class. They come in many different formats; some count on, while others count down. They can display minutes, seconds, or both. There are many visual options to choose from as well.

> **TIP** When you find a few online timers that you like, bookmark them so you can easily find them when you need them. Avoid anything overly distracting when students are expected to be working. When you don't require the students to be as focused (e.g., during free time or during an indoor recess), feel free to be as fun and creative with your timer as you'd like.

Individual Timers versus Whole Class Timers

The decision to use a timer with individual students or with the whole class may depend on several variables. The student may feel that an individual timer singles them out or draws unwanted attention to them. A whole class timer may highlight how quickly some finish and emphasize how much longer it takes other students. This may foster a feeling of defeat or failure, or may cause negative competition. These possibilities may be activity-dependent and there may be some activities that you feel an individual timer would be best, and others that you feel would be better served by a whole class timer. You know your student and your class dynamics best.

There may be some activities that you feel an individual timer would be best, and others that you feel would be better served by a whole class timer.

Using a Timer for Reinforcement

We discussed the importance of reinforcement in Chapter 6. Timers can be used to motivate and engage students, and they can also provide reinforcement opportunities. When students are motivated, you will see an increase in their level of engagement, their attitude, and their achievement.

A Set Amount of Time

One of the most basic uses of a timer is to set an expectation for how long the student is expected to work

One of the most basic uses of a timer is to set an expectation for how long the student is expected to work. Similar to a first/then strategy, the student earns access to reinforcement by working for the expected amount of time. In this approach, it would be important to start at an attainable amount of time (i.e., a duration the student is already able to meet) and then gradually increase the length of time. As we discussed earlier, this allows the student to achieve success immediately and increases their level of buy-in. This is very similar to the approach many teachers use to build reading stamina in their classrooms.

Building on this approach is the strategy of giving the student a set amount of time (slightly more time than the student would/should require) and allowing the student to use any remaining time on the timer for an activity of their choosing. In this way, the student is motivated to complete their task quickly to maximize the amount of time they have for their activity of choice. Depending on the student and the activity, it may be important to set work quality expectations as you don't want them to rush through the activity carelessly just to get it completed. Having said this, if the student has never produced/completed much work, you may choose to tackle quality later. You are in the best position to determine this.

Modifying this approach slightly, you might give the student a set amount of time (again more time than the student would/should require) and allow the student to "bank" any unused minutes. These minutes could be accumulated to earn a larger reinforcer at a later time. If you are considering this approach, try using a minute-for-minute value. If the student would like an extra recess for the class, a 15-minute recess would require 15 earned (or banked) minutes. Students can be very motivated using this approach, especially depending on what they might be able to "buy" with their minutes. For example, the student could save up minutes to buy a 20-minute TV episode for the class. The class watches this while they eat lunch so there is no issue with loss of instructional time, and the student who earns the reward also earns some positive peer attention, which is always a bonus.

With this approach there is also the possibility of having multiple students, or the whole class for that matter, bank minutes toward full-class rewards. Because they will be earning minutes at a faster rate, you might want to put a price on various rewards (so not a minute-for-minute value). Consider factors like how quickly you think they will accumulate rewards and if the rewards will impact time on task. If you are doing this with the whole class, try creating the list of possible rewards together with students and then negotiating a fair number of minutes required to earn each reward.

When earning future rewards, be mindful that the rewards need to be reasonably accessible and the amount of time it will take students to earn a reward also needs to be reasonable. Students may be motivated at the start of the school year to earn a blockbuster movie for the class, but this may feel hopeless if Thanksgiving has come and gone and they are just over halfway to their goal. This also creates the potential risk of some students giving up while others still really want the movie to happen. In this situation there may be some negative peer interactions between those students still striving to earn minutes and those who have given up. Make sure not to create a situation that results in negative peer attention or interactions.

Self-Competition

Some timer strategies work well with students motivated by self-competition. In this approach, students do not risk embarrassment or unwanted peer attention as they are not competing with their peers. In a self-competition approach, the student works to beat their own score. One obvious strategy is for the student to beat their score in relation to time. For example, if a task took them 12 minutes on Tuesday, let's see if they can get it done in under 12 minutes on Wednesday (even by seconds), then less on Thursday, etc. It will be important to make sure the student is able to meet success in this activity. If beating their score on a daily basis is not reasonable, perhaps they could decrease their time from week to week, or decrease their weekly total. Adapt this strategy to meet the needs of your student to ensure they are successful.

Another option is not to compete with their time, but rather with the quantity of work they can complete during a set amount of time. For instance, writing is an area many students struggle with and (consequently?) dislike. Consider the following example:

Karlotta has been working with a timer for writing tasks. Initially you started her off with two minutes and have gradually increased her time to ten minutes. Instead of continuing to increase the amount of time she writes for, look at increasing the amount of writing she completes in that amount of time. If Karlotta has written three sentences in ten minutes, look at reinforcing her for writing more than three sentences in ten minutes. Then continue to increase her output—"beating her own score," so to speak.

Some timer strategies work well with students motivated by self-competition.

Some students are motivated by discussing what is expected of them in terms of the task and then having them predict how long it will take them to complete the task. The student could then receive reinforcement for completing the task within the predicted amount of time, or for task completion regardless of time. If the student is motivated to predict their time and see how close they come to meeting their prediction, let that be motivating in and of itself. You can reinforce task completion, as this is the ultimate goal anyway. For this strategy to be effective for the student, they would need to have a basic understanding of time, as well as their own abilities and productivity. If you use this strategy, it can be useful to look back at other similar tasks and their times to help the student make an accurate predication.

> **TIP** To track the amount of time it takes to complete various tasks, try recording the time at the top of the page. It would also be beneficial to chart the data.

Other Ways to Use Timers

You can use timers in many other ways for behavior management. One example is "angry/sad time." Consider Sagar, a boy in the primary grades:

> Sagar is very quirky and dramatic, and his moods often sidetrack his productivity. He often shares with you that he is unable to work because he is angry or sad. Most of the time there are no precipitating factors—no one says or does anything to make him feel this way. Instead, he feels these moods emerge and they consequently prevent him from working.
>
> After countless attempts to resolve any issues, you give in to Sagar's rationale that he just needs to have these feelings. You give him a timer and says, "Okay, I have set the timer for two minutes. You have two minutes to be angry." To your surprise (and relief), when the timer beeps, Sagar brings the timer to you, smiles, and is ready to work. This two-minute timer becomes a regular routine for Sagar and works successfully for the remainder of the year.

One other strategy that can be very powerful is the 30-second strategy. It can be easy to fall into a power struggle with a student, especially when you feel they are not complying. And the more adamant you become, the more resistant the student may become. Thirty seconds can turn this around. If you have a student who is often slow to comply, allow them 30 seconds. Some students aren't actually refusing to comply, but instead may need more time than you expect. And when you are frustrated, you don't always have an accurate gauge of the seconds/minutes that are passing. Keep a 30-second timer available (or even a minute timer) that you can use when needed.

Many non-compliers may just be slow to comply.

Many non-compliers may just be slow to comply. By providing them with some time between your initial direction and a possible re-direction (which may be elevated or which they may interpret as nagging or embarrassing), you are allowing them time to process the request and to feel as though they are complying on their own terms. This is important for the student and for your relationship with the student. And if the student is already having a bad day, add another 10–15 seconds. This can make a huge difference.

When using a timer with students, you can always find some reason to reward them with bonus minutes or bonus time when needed. We all have bad days, and ensuring your students meet success and have access to reinforcement is even more important on the bad days than on the good ones. If you can find a reason to say "You did such a great job on _____ yesterday that I am giving you two bonus minutes today!" it may make a world of difference for the student.

KEY IDEAS

- Timers can be an excellent tool to support behavior management.
- There are many kinds of timers, including sand timers, wind up timers, and digital timers.
- You can use timers with individual students or with the whole class.
- Timers can be used to motivate and engage students, and they can also provide reinforcement opportunities.
- One of the most basic uses of a timer is to set an expectation for how long the student is expected to work.
- With a self-competition approach to timers, the student works to beat their own score.
- Another option is for the student to compete with the quantity of work they can complete during a set amount of time.
- You can use timers in many other ways for behavior management.

11

Addressing Other Challenging Behavior

With running and SIB, the things that maintain the behavior may not be within your control, making them even more challenging.

In this book we have explored the complexities of behavior and why behaviors occur. Some of the most challenging behaviors are running and self-injurious behaviors (SIB). We have looked at things that maintain behaviors, typically what a student "gets" or "avoids" by engaging in the behavior. These, for the most part, are within your control—even if you don't realize it at the time. With running and SIB, the things that maintain the behavior may not be within your control, making them even more challenging. Instead, the behaviors are almost self-maintained.

Running

When a student runs, either away from a staff member or from an area, you are obligated to follow them to ensure their safety. If the student is aware that you are following them, this can turn into a fun game of chase for the student. There is often nothing more motivating than this game of chase, and you can't stop the game by not following the student as the student must be supervised.

The best recommendation for this behavior is to not run after the student. If you are able to monitor the student (maintaining visual contact) without following them, this would be ideal. But this is often not possible. In this circumstance, follow the student, but don't actively run. Following the student without running makes it less likely that the student will think you are chasing them. This gets tricky around corners or stairs as it is imperative that you know where the student is at all times. At these times, you may need to run to make sure you don't lose visual contact. If possible, run without the student seeing you. However, there may be times when the student will see you running. Although you run the risk of looking like you are playing chase at these times, sometimes there is no way to avoid this. In addition, avoid making eye contact with the student while you are following them as it supports the notion that you are playing with them.

So, what can you do to try to prevent running behavior? Here are some suggestions:

- If the student sits close to the door in class, move the student's desk/seat as far away from the door as possible. This will give you a visual heads up if/when the student leaves the room as they will have to cross the classroom instead of just slipping out the door.
- If you can identify specific times of day when the student tends to run, try altering the schedule if possible so the student is engaged in a high-preference activity at that time.
- If you know the student tends to run during transition times, identify an activity you could do with the student to distract and engage them as you transition from one activity to another. For instance:
  ○ Have the student be the leader.
  ○ Give the student an errand to do on the way to the destination (e.g., deliver something to the office).
  ○ Give the student immediate access to a reinforcer for arriving at the destination without running.
  ○ Gently toss a ball back and forth with the student while walking.
  ○ Play follow the leader with a support staff or peer buddy, twisting, turning, jumping, or skipping while walking to the destination.
  ○ Allow the student to push a toy car to the destination on their hands and knees.

> **TIP** Some of these suggestions may seem odd, but they often work. It will be up to you (and the school team if applicable) to determine if the benefit of having the student not run outweighs the odd nature of these activities.

- If you can identify anything more motivating to the student than running, use that to redirect the student when they are running.
- Make following the student as un-fun as possible. Give the student as little direct attention as possible (e.g., limited dialogue, limited eye-contact, attempt to appear as though you are not following/chasing).
- Offer chase as a reinforcer for other opportunities throughout the day and be as fun and interactive as you can when chase is earned. This will help motivate the student to "earn the fun chase" versus have the less fun experience you create when they run without permission.
- If the student has been earning chase and liking that experience, try to redirect any un-earned running by saying something like, "If you want me to play chase with you, we will need to finish our book first." If the student appears to consider this option, continue to prompt. If the student continues to run, discontinue dialogue as you don't want the student to perceive this as active engagement.
- Do not give a lot of attention to the behavior after it is over. Redirect if/as necessary, but do not spend a lot of time discussing the running as attention to and about the behavior may be reinforcing.
- Depending on the layout and context of your building and the needs of your student, you might need support. If your student runs at identifiable times, you may require a staff member to be in a certain location at a certain time

to help monitor the student and ensure they do not go outside or to any unsafe locations within the building.

- Use a walkie talkie or another form of communication if/when the student runs. Discuss with your school team who would be the best person to communicate with (e.g., guidance, resource, admin, etc.). Communication is key if you are unable to keep up with the student, if they are out of your sight, if you have to follow the student outside, etc.
- If the student leaves school property, you may need to have someone contact the parents and possibly the police depending on the age of the student and the context of the situation. Follow the direction provided in the student's behavior plan (if applicable) and any board/district policies for such situations.

Given the severity of running and the difficulty in eliminating this behavior, offer big reinforcers at the start.

Given the severity of running and the difficulty in eliminating this behavior, offer big reinforcers at the start. When dealing with situations that could involve safety, start by offering whatever is necessary to address the behavior and then gradually fade it out. Collaborate with the school team (if your school has one), administration, resource teachers, other supports, and parents. Everyone will need to be on the same page with the plan in place to address this behavior.

Self-Injurious Behavior (SIB)

You cannot ignore a behavior that causes harm or injury to a student.

SIB is another type of behavior that many find challenging. One reason is that you are compelled to give attention to this behavior. You cannot ignore a behavior that causes harm or injury to a student. The other potential issue, which is also problematic, is that SIB may be reinforced on a sensory level, making it potentially very difficult to re-create in a positive and appropriate way.

> **TIP** Some SIB may be related to mental health distress and may require the support of medical and/or mental health professionals (e.g., cutting). When dealing with SIB of any kind, ensure that all appropriate support people are involved in creating a plan to appropriately support the student. It is not uncommon to have multiple support people involved in cases dealing with SIB.

Consider the following case study of severe SIB:

Roberto repeatedly punches himself in the head with a closed fist. He has a disability that impacts his cognitive ability, and he is not able to verbally communicate. Given this, it is very difficult to determine the function of the behavior. Roberto engages in this behavior almost continuously throughout the day. It is determined that this behavior is not triggered by any external factors as it occurs across all contexts of Roberto's day.

It is painful for teachers and support staff to see Roberto punching himself. He is beginning to lose his hair where he punches, and his doctor is concerned that brain damage may result from his SIB. Eliminating this behavior is crucial, or, at the very least, reducing the damage caused by the behavior.

To stop this behavior, staff members attempt to physically prevent Roberto from punching himself by trying to hold his hand away from his head. This is not successful as he is very strong. They then attempt to hold Roberto's hand against his head, rubbing his head with his closed fist. The hope was that this might provide sensory stimulation (possibly even feel better than the punching) that could replace the punching. This too is ineffective.

Some staff feel that calming Roberto down might reduce these behaviors. They speak to him in a soft and soothing voice while he punches himself, trying to gently guide his arm away. This is also unsuccessful and, based on data, appears to increase the behavior.

Data becomes very important in attempting to address the behavior. Anecdotal data collected by one of the consultants involved in supporting this student reveals some helpful patterns. Rob vocalizes less and engages in SIB less when working with one specific support staff. Although he still engages in the behavior, it occurs less frequently and with less intensity. After noting this pattern in the data, the teacher observes Roberto with all of his support staff to identify differences in their approaches. The staff member with whom the reduction in SIB is noted is very approachable. He talks and interacts with Roberto as he would with any other student, he speaks in a regular volume, and when Roberto engages in SIB the staff member redirects Roberto using the same voice that he uses in his other interactions with the student.

It is difficult to determine if these are the reasons Roberto's SIB is lower with this staff member. It might be because this staff member is male and perhaps Roberto has more positive experiences with males than females in other contexts of his life. These are things that may never be determined. Either way, the plan for Roberto tries to capitalize on the characteristics observed with this staff member, and schedules are rearranged to increase Roberto's time with this staff member.

Despite rigorous and frequent review of data, and endless attempts to tweak the plan, Roberto continues to engage in SIB. The reduced frequency and intensity are not enough to eliminate the risk of brain damage. Roberto eventually must wear a helmet to prevent brain damage. This case study highlights the very complex nature of SIB.

Here is another example of a non-verbal student with a cognitive disability who exhibits SIB:

Amelia bites the middle knuckle on her pointer finger. Her finger is very swollen and callused due to the frequent and repeated biting. The teacher observes Amelia multiple times and records data related to her knuckle biting behavior. This behavior appears to be a self-stimulatory behavior and is not related to specific triggers. She engages in this behavior when she is excited, angry, happy, or sad. The teacher attempts to put in a verbal re-direct paired with a visual, but these are unsuccessful. The teacher also tries giving her something else to bite (e.g., gum, a pencil chew-topper, chewy candy) but this too is unsuccessful.

Next, the teacher tries making Amelia a ring to wear using crafting foam. The ring is very big, so it covers almost the full area between her bottom and middle knuckle. The rationale for this is two-fold: first, the teacher hopes the ring will be a deterrent for biting by feeling weird and displeasing in her mouth. Second, the teacher thinks the gentle pressure on her finger might be pleasing. Remember, the teacher is not sure if it is the feeling of the bite in her mouth or the feeling of the bite on her finger that might be maintaining the behavior.

The ring works! Amelia does not bite her finger when wearing the ring, and she doesn't seem to mind wearing the ring. After several weeks, the teacher begins to reduce the size of the ring very slowly. Over the course of several months the ring becomes the size of a regular band.

As these examples show, SIB cases can be very complex. As a result, the involvement of outside support is critical when dealing with SIB. Remember, SIB is bigger than any one individual. If you have a student exhibiting SIB, seek help.

Reducing expectations and/ or increasing reinforcement is a proactive approach to supporting your student when they are having a bad day

| **TIP** | Regardless of what strategy you are using or how well your student may be doing, remember that you may need to reduce expectations and increase opportunities for your student to access reinforcement during stressful times. Reducing expectations and/or increasing reinforcement is a proactive approach to supporting your student when they are having a bad day. |

KEY IDEAS

- Some of the most challenging behaviors are running and self-injurious behaviors (SIB).
- For running and SIB, the things that maintain the behavior may not be within your control.
- There are various strategies you can use to prevent running behavior from occuring.
- Given the severity of running and the difficulty in eliminating this behavior, offer big reinforcers at the start.
- SIB may be reinforced on a sensory level, making it potentially very difficult to re-create in a positive and appropriate way.
- When dealing with SIB of any kind, ensure that all appropriate support people are involved in creating a plan to appropriately support the student.

12

··

Conclusion

By understanding that behaviors are complex and that behavior management is not an easy task, we give ourselves permission to make mistakes—and that's okay!

I began this book by stating that behaviors are very complex, and I will end the book in the same way. By understanding that behaviors are complex and that behavior management is not an easy task, we give ourselves permission to make mistakes—and that's okay! No two behaviors are the same, and this means that often the strategies that work for one student, or in one situation, may not work for another student or in a different situation. For this, and many other reasons, managing student behavior can be overwhelming.

It is important to take care of yourself so you can remain positive and practical when dealing with challenging behaviors. And remember, the rest of your class will follow your lead in terms of how you respond to challenging behaviors. When the plans and strategies don't work on a given day and a student storms out of your classroom throwing books and dropping an f-bomb as they leave, your reaction will model regulation for the students in your class. It is okay to show empathy for students who are struggling. When you are able to see your challenging students as students who are struggling, you are better able to be empathetic and compassionate when dealing with their behaviors.

As an administrator, I have had the opportunity to work with our most challenging students. And although they are often sent to the office for punitive reasons, I am always mindful to keep my interactions positive and productive. Students often reach their behavioral peak as they get to the office, so I have been on the receiving end of some very colorful language, desk slamming, chair throwing, and more.

Despite these behaviors, I have developed very strong relationships with these students and we have been able to create a positive rapport. This doesn't mean they no longer get sent to the office or that they no longer flip their lids when they get there; rather, it means they trust me enough to flip their lids and know they will not be judged because of it. They trust that I will support them as best as I can, even though there are times I am not sure what to say or what to do, and they engage more readily in relationship rebuilding with me following a meltdown.

In fact, our most challenging students have become some of my most favorite students. This may be due to the amount of time I have spent with them, the value of the relationship we have built (knowing the level of trust and respect this required from them), and the empathy I have developed as I gained an understanding of everything they were trying to balance in their lives. Regardless, these students have secured a special place in my heart.

Consider the following example. At the end of one school year, a Grade 6 student mentioned how much they thought I was going to miss them. Another student chimed in to add, "I bet you aren't going to miss Arthur!" A few students giggled at this comment. Arthur, of course, was the most challenging student in the class. Because of his explosive behaviors over the years, his peers were aware of how many times he had been sent to the office.

"Actually," I responded, "Wouldn't it make sense that I'd miss him the most?" The students stopped giggling and looked at me. "After all," I said, "He and I have spent the most time together." Arthur raised his head and looked at me. I smiled at him, and he smiled back at me. And truth be told, I would miss him when he was gone.

I often think of Arthur and hope he is continuing to experience success as he progresses through his school years. I am sure he will have meltdowns as he was dealing with a lot of issues which I am certain have not gone away. But with supports and strategies in place, he was able to have more good days than bad. I hope that pattern continued for him.

Arthur's story would certainly encompass the entirety of this book. His behaviors were extreme beginning in Grade 1, and continued to peak until Grade 4. His Grade 5 and 6 years were markedly better due to all the support he received. His support team consisted of teachers, resource teachers, guidance, administration, his mother, and outside services including a pediatrician and community services. His behavior plan included all areas: medical, academic, behavioral, social-emotional, relationships, skill building, sensory, and work jobs.

Arthur was a complex student although he did not have any specific diagnosis. He was also funny, likeable, and always willing to help. When Arthur was having a good day, he could be the sweetest, most thoughtful student you have ever met. He responded well to praise and success, and wanted desperately to have positive friendships. When we focused on these positives, it was easier to build rapport with him, especially if I kept these things in mind during his meltdowns.

Arthur had a good skill set in math but struggled with reading and writing, which sometimes became an issue in math class (which was what I was teaching). During the school year, I saw Arthur throw his desk multiple times and storm out of class. When he returned, I would offer to catch him up on what we had covered while he was out of the classroom. He always chose to come to the front of the room and work with me either at my desk or on the whiteboard if there was space there for him to work. I was always fine with this as it was his way to verify our relationship was still intact. It was also a great way for the class to see that he was calm and that things were not uncomfortable.

There were days when he would approach me, before any desk throwing occurred, and ask if he could work at my desk or on the whiteboard. Very rarely would I have any reason to say no to this request. He worked very well in those locations and I was able to build on those occasions to have him help other students who were struggling with math as they were close enough for me to monitor. This helped build his confidence in math as well as develop positive interactions and relationships with his peers.

Because Arthur was experiencing success in school, our relationship with his family strengthened as well. We came to a point where his mother would offer to keep him home on days we had a substitute teacher in our class if she felt he would not be able to handle that challenge on a particular day. Because of some of Arthur's challenges, we always tried to secure a substitute teacher who had a positive rapport with him. However when this was not possible, having him stay home was extremely beneficial.as it helped maintain his level of success and allowed him to avoid unnecessary hardships that we knew were outside of his skillset to handle. This eventually evolved into Arthur being able to come to school with an unknown or non-preferred substitute, trusting that he could choose to work in the office if he felt things were not going well. This level of independence and self-awareness were excellent accomplishments for Arthur.

Over the years countless strategies, plans, and programs were put in place to support Arthur, including BSPs, strategies, visuals, academic adaptations, resource interventions, guidance programs, social skills programs, multiple reinforcement systems, various work jobs, and peer mentoring (as peer and as mentor with support), to name a few. Many data charts were also created to illustrate the success, or lack thereof, of these strategies and programs.

When progress is slow, it is important to look for and celebrate the smallest of accomplishments.

It is important to keep in mind that success is not immediate, and for Arthur this was certainly the case. Some issues may be tackled quickly, but others can take a significant amount of time. As we stated in the section on childhood trauma, there are some things that can take months and even years to accomplish. When progress is slow, it is important to look for and celebrate the smallest of accomplishments. A success is a success, no matter how small. And education is all about celebrating and capitalizing on success.

Remember, behavior difficulties are challenging. But you are not alone. Rely on your school team for help and support. Let your data drive your decisions. And develop a rapport with your students. With these as your starting points, you will be heading in the right direction.

Recommended Resources

Books:

Carrington, Jody. 2020. *Kids These Days: A Game Plan for (Re)Connecting with Those We Teach, Lead, & Love.* Impress.

Carrington, Jody, and Laurie McIntosh. 2021. *Teachers These Days: Stories and Strategies for Reconnection.* Impress.

Greene, Ross W. 2014. *Lost at School: Why Our Kids with Behavioral Challenges are Falling Through the Cracks and How We Can Help Them.* Scribner.

Information about adverse childhood experiences and childhood trauma:

- Center on the Developing Child, Harvard University website. ACEs and Toxic Stress, online resource: https://developingchild.harvard.edu/resources/aces-and-toxic-stress-frequently-asked-questions/
- Centers for Disease Control and Prevention website: https://www.cdc.gov/violenceprevention/aces/fastfact.html
- Schulman, Meryl and Alexandra Maul. Screening for Adverse Childhood Experiences and Trauma. Center for Health CareStrategies. Available: https://www.chcs.org/media/TA-Tool-Screening-for-ACEs-and-Trauma_020619.pdf
- Adverse Childhood Experience Questionnaire: https://www.theannainstitute.org/Finding%20Your%20ACE%20Score.pdf
- The National Child Traumatic Stress Network website: https://www.nctsn.org/what-is-child-trauma/trauma-types

Examples of behavior contract templates:

- https://k12engagement.unl.edu/strategy-briefs/Behavior%20Contracting%201-20-2014.pdf
- https://achieve.lausd.net/cms/lib/CA01000043/Centricity/domain/361/positive%20behavior/tier%20ii/t2%20resources/The%205%20Ws%20of%20Behavior%20Contracting.pdf

Information about emotional regulation:

- Focus on Self-Regulation online resource: https://www.ecsd.net/page/1833/focus-on-self-regulation
- Zones of regulation website: https://www.zonesofregulation.com/index.html
- Kuypers, Leah. 2011. *The Zones of Regulation.* Think Social Publishing.

- Stuart Shanker. 2016. *Self-Reg: How to Help Your Child (and You) Break the Stress Cycle and Successfully Engage with Life.* Viking.
- Buie, Amy. 2016. *Rage to Reason.* Online resource: https://mjja.org/images/training/conferences/2016/spring/presentations/rage-to-reason.pdf

Examples of forced choice surveys (preference surveys):
- https://content.schoolinsites.com/api/documents/0993c53781524334a3bc5bb1391e8f66.pdf
- https://autismteachingsupports.weebly.com/uploads/5/5/9/7/55979461/reinforcement_and_preference_interview-_sentence_completion_portion.pdf
- https://www.mayinstitute.org/pdfs/presentations/PBIS2019-T-A3C-Preference%20Assessment%20Packet.pdf

Examples of data collection templates for ABC data:
- https://autismclassroomresources.com/collecting-abc-data-freebie-in-step-2/
- https://www.templateroller.com/template/345440/antecedent-behavior-consequence-abc-data-collection-form.html
- https://blogs.sd41.bc.ca/lss/resource-centre/data-collection/

Examples of data collection templates for frequency data:
- https://www.templateroller.com/template/268458/event-frequency-data-sheet-multiple-behaviors-and-dates.html
- https://i.pinimg.com/originals/10/40/75/104075a498d511f1f4406f099a614dad.jpg

Information about visuals/social stories:
- SETbc website: https://www.setbc.org
- Head Start Center for Inclusion website: https://headstartinclusion.org
- Carol Gray Social Stories website: https://carolgraysocialstories.com/social-stories/social-story-sampler/
- Happy Learners website: https://happylearners.info/social-stories/

Appendix

Sample Data Collection Chart

Student:

Direction:

Date/Time	Antecedent	Behavior	Consequence	Initials

Pembroke Publishers ©2022 *Managing Student Behavior: how to identify, understand, and defuse challenging classroom situations* by Marsha Costello ISBN 978-1-55138-355-2

Sample Data Collection Checklist

Student:
Direction:

Date/Time	Antecedent	Behavior	Consequence	Initials
	☐ presented with non-preferred task (_____) ☐ asked to stop a preferred activity (_____) ☐ coming in from outside ☐ entering/leaving music/gym ☐ other: _____ _____		☐ task/demand removed ☐ taken to sensory room ☐ sent home ☐ guidance/resource ☐ other: _____ _____	

Date/Time	Antecedent	Behavior	Consequence	Initials
	☐ presented with non-preferred task (_____) ☐ asked to stop a preferred activity (_____) ☐ coming in from outside ☐ entering/leaving music/gym ☐ other: _____ _____		☐ task/demand removed ☐ taken to sensory room ☐ sent home ☐ guidance/resource ☐ other: _____ _____	

Date/Time	Antecedent	Behavior	Consequence	Initials
	☐ presented with non-preferred task (_____) ☐ asked to stop a preferred activity (_____) ☐ coming in from outside ☐ entering/leaving music/gym ☐ other: _____ _____		☐ task/demand removed ☐ taken to sensory room ☐ sent home ☐ guidance/resource ☐ other: _____ _____	

Sample Tally Chart (30 minute increments)

Student:

Direction:

Date:

9:00–9:30	9:30–10:00	10:00–10:30	10:30–11:00	11:00–11:30	11:30–12:00	12:00–12:30	12:30–1:00	1:00–1:30	1:30–2:00	2:00–2:30	2:30–3:00

Pembroke Publishers ©2022 *Managing Student Behavior: how to identify, understand, and defuse challenging classroom situations* by Marsha Costello ISBN 978-1-55138-355-2

Sample Tally Chart (15 minute increments – morning)

Student:

Direction:

Date:	9:00–9:15	9:15–9:30	9:30–9:45	9:45–10:00	10:00–10:15	10:15–10:30	10:30–10:45	10:45–11:00	11:00–11:15	11:15–11:30	11:30–11:45	11:45–12:00

Pembroke Publishers ©2022 *Managing Student Behavior: how to identify, understand, and defuse challenging classroom situations* by Marsha Costello ISBN 978-1-55138-355-2

Sample Tally Chart (15 minute increments – afternoon)

Student:

Direction:

Date:

12:00–12:15	12:15–12:30	12:30–12:45	12:45–1:00	1:00–1:15	1:15–1:30	1:30–1:45	1:45–2:00	2:00–2:15	2:15–2:30	2:30–2:45	2:45–3:00

Pembroke Publishers ©2022 *Managing Student Behavior: how to identify, understand, and defuse challenging classroom situations* by Marsha Costello ISBN 978-1-55138-355-2

Sample Tally Chart (blank)

Student:

Direction:

Date:

Pembroke Publishers ©2022 *Managing Student Behavior: how to identify, understand, and defuse challenging classroom situations* by Marsha Costello ISBN 978-1-55138-355-2

Sample Chart of Frequency Data

Student:

Targeted Behavior:

Date														
Day	Mon	Tues	Wed	Thurs	Fri	Mon	Tues	Wed	Thurs	Fri	Mon	Tues	Wed	Thurs	Fri
1														
2														
3														
4														
5														
6														
7														
8														
9														
10														

Pembroke Publishers ©2022 *Managing Student Behavior: how to identify, understand, and defuse challenging classroom situations* by Marsha Costello ISBN 978-1-55138-355-2

Sample Chart of Frequency Data (Blank)

Student:

Targeted Behavior:

Day	Mon	Tues	Wed	Thurs	Fri	Mon	Tues	Wed	Thurs	Fri	Mon	Tues	Wed	Thurs	Fri
Date															

Pembroke Publishers ©2022 *Managing Student Behavior: how to identify, understand, and defuse challenging classroom situations* by Marsha Costello ISBN 978-1-55138-355-2

Index